My Voyage to America

The Diary of Rudolph Braëm
a Danish Merchant
1829–1831

My Voyage to America

The Diary of Rudolph Braëm,
a Danish Merchant, 1829–1831

ISBN: 9780578750064

For reprint, order, or sales information, please contact:

Donald Valade
dvalade@truvisglobal.com

Printed in the United States of America

Acknowledgment

*Many thanks to our
Onkel Steen Vedel,
whose passion, guidance, and love
made this historical journey
through time come to life.*

Foreword

In the year 1829, our Danish forefather Rudolph Braëm sailed from Le Havre, France to the new country, the United States of America, at the port of New Orleans. He spent two years traveling the North American continent and being a very educated young man kept a diary of all what he did and observed. It is a fascinating and delightful read which has never before been made available to the public. I believe historians of this period will be very pleased to find another source, so vibrant and detailed, for this period in our American history. Rudolph writes about the debutantes of New Orleans, the debauchery and dangers of Mexico, American enslavement, and his adventures while traveling North along the Mississippi River.

Now, after 189 years and six generations of family in Denmark, his diary has again returned to America to reside with his American descendants who are many and proud to share his story.

Donald Valade

Rudolph Gothard Sigvart Braëm
December 23, 1801 — October 15, 1838

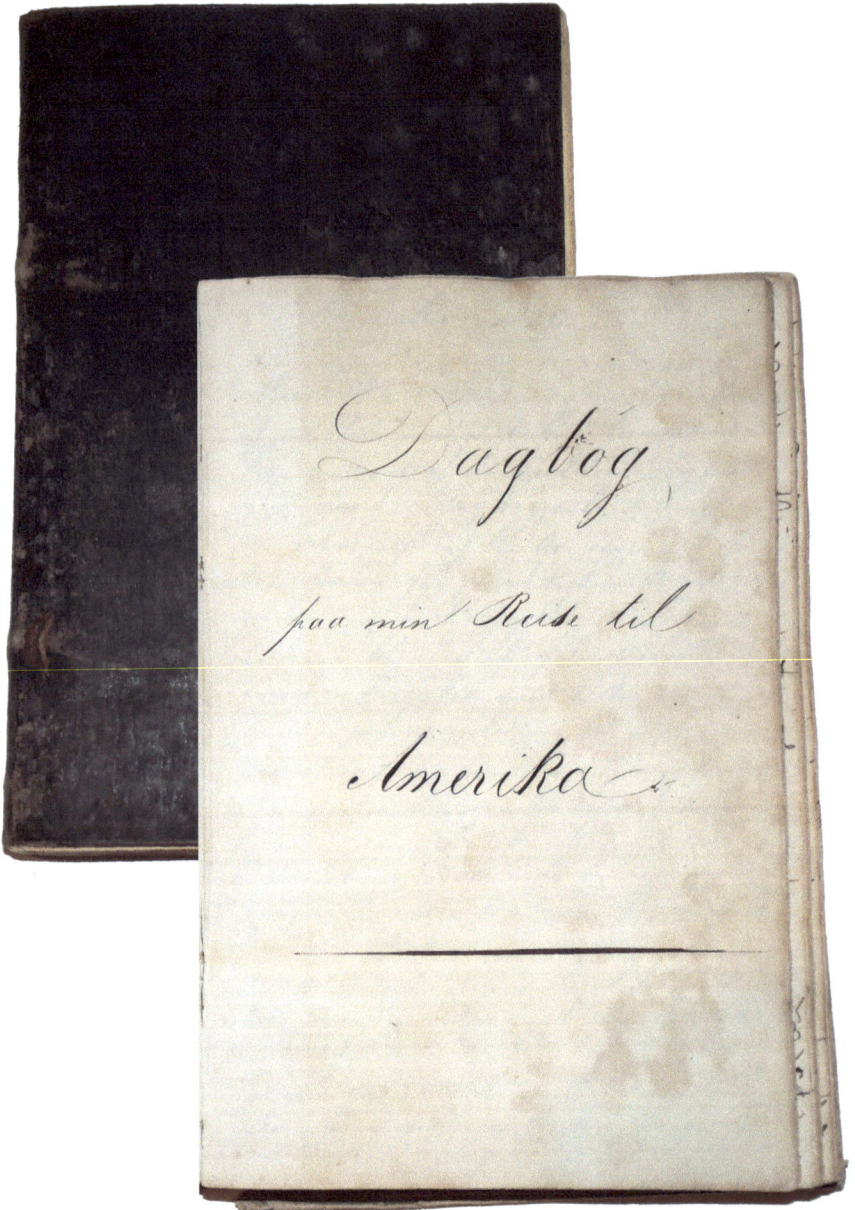

**Rudolph Braëm's Diary
"My Journey to America"**

The Voyage to America

I n the year 1829, I have seen more of our globe than in all my previous lifespan, and it has been one of the most extraordinary years of my experience. I began the year — after 6½ years' absence — at home surrounded by those which heaven gave me dearest on earth and was there occupied with preparations for a journey round the entire Baltic, which I would make in the company of two friends.

On the 13th of January, I left for that purpose Copenhagen and arrived in Hamburg on the 17th, and continued on the 25th along the coast, visiting Lübeck, Wismar, Rostock, Stralsund, Greifswald, Arkona, Stettin, Danzig, Elbing, Königsberg, and Memel; we then crossed the Russian frontier on March 1· and arrived in the capital of the great empire on March 15, after having touched on Libau and Riga. After a fortnight's stay and admiration of the sights, we left St. Petersburg on March 31, and took the road via Wiborg, Frederikshamn, Lovisa, and Borg on to Helsingfors, where I took leave of my travel companions, who continued over Torneaa while I took a rest after first having visited the only copper mine in Finland.

On April 15, I crossed on the ice over to Sweden and arrived on the 16th in Stockholm, where I only stayed three days, and was on the 28th in the town of Ystad. By the first available steamer, I crossed the next day over to Greifswald and continued along the coast of Pomerania and Mecklenburg to Hamburg, where it was my intention to spend the summer. This did not rule out that I went to see my relatives over in Whitsun, but I returned immediately and remained in Hamburg until September 12. Following instructions from my employers in Le Havre, I then returned via Amsterdam, Antwerp, Gent, Lille, Amiens and Rouen, and arrived in Le Havre on September 23.

I have thus this year traversed a great deal of northern Europe, but the year would not come to an end before I had seen another continent, and it was not without satisfaction that, upon my arrival in Le Havre, I received my new orders: to leave for the United States by the first available ship, which sailed to New Orleans, and from there, in all probability, cross over to Tampico on the Mexican coast in order to sort out a difficult business problem concerning my company.

A ship was ready to leave a fortnight later. Although before my departure from Hamburg I had already been expecting to make a journey to America, I had not been able to assume that the destination would be other than New York, and this new turn of events did, therefore, surprise me, especially as it was coupled with such a hasty departure. I did not, however, hesitate a moment in accepting an offer which could be just as useful as it was rewarding to my self-esteem.

The ship, *America*, under command of Capt. Kittson, was that upon which my passage should take place in the company of many other passengers whom I shall describe further. My several or numerous preparations that were necessitated by such a considerable journey made the already short time even shorter. We had, however, the annoyance which has been the lot of so many travelers — especially in Le Havre — namely, that the wind was contrary on the day of departure and also on the next and even for another three days. But this must, under the circumstances, be considered luck, when one knows that ships sometimes, especially this time of year, can lie three to four weeks waiting for a fair wind, to the great distress of the poor travelers and the great joy of the innkeepers, who in truth can be said to live off the wind, particularly if it blows from the southwest, which generally happens nine months of the year.

Finally, on October 15, the wind veered to the northwest, and the *America* did not waste much time in taking advantage of a change for the better. We thus sailed, although many with me thought that we lacked the signs of stability in this better direction of the wind. However, as busy as I was in these last moments, I cannot deny that I felt quite apprehensive the whole day of departure. It gives one a strange feeling to embark upon a sea voyage where one, mayhap for three months, will see nothing but the sky and the sea. The thought of the various events which such a voyage will present and of the consequences for one's whole life on which it may be influenced is also of a nature to elicit a special state of mind.

In my cabin alone are twenty passengers, and on the lower deck about fifty, partly emigrants from Alsace and Lorraine, so one would not suffer from lack of company, but perhaps not either all sorts of unpleasantness, as is usually the result of the close proximity of so many diverse characters in everyday communication. The worst fear was the danger to our health caused by the confined space where all the poor people with women and children had to be housed. The odors in a warm climate could prove to be not only unpleasant, but also directly dangerous, even to us. Luckily, this fear was unfounded just as was the even more realistic fear that we would not have water enough for this multitude of people, although our passage turned out to take longer time than we had hoped.

For the fare of 750 francs per passenger in the cabin, the captain had made ample and excellent provisions. He had also taken on board, apart from a great number of chickens, ducks, geese and turkeys, fourteen sheep and a number of pigs, so we had fresh meat during the whole journey, and altogether a table, which only in a few respects reminded us of the fact that we were several hundred miles away from shore. Every Thursday, in commemoration of our departure, which happened on that day, and every Sunday we drank as much champagne as we wished, and on the other days, we had, apart from ordinary table wine, burgundy and Madeira. For me, this was no pleasure, as I liked wine no better at sea than I did on dry land.

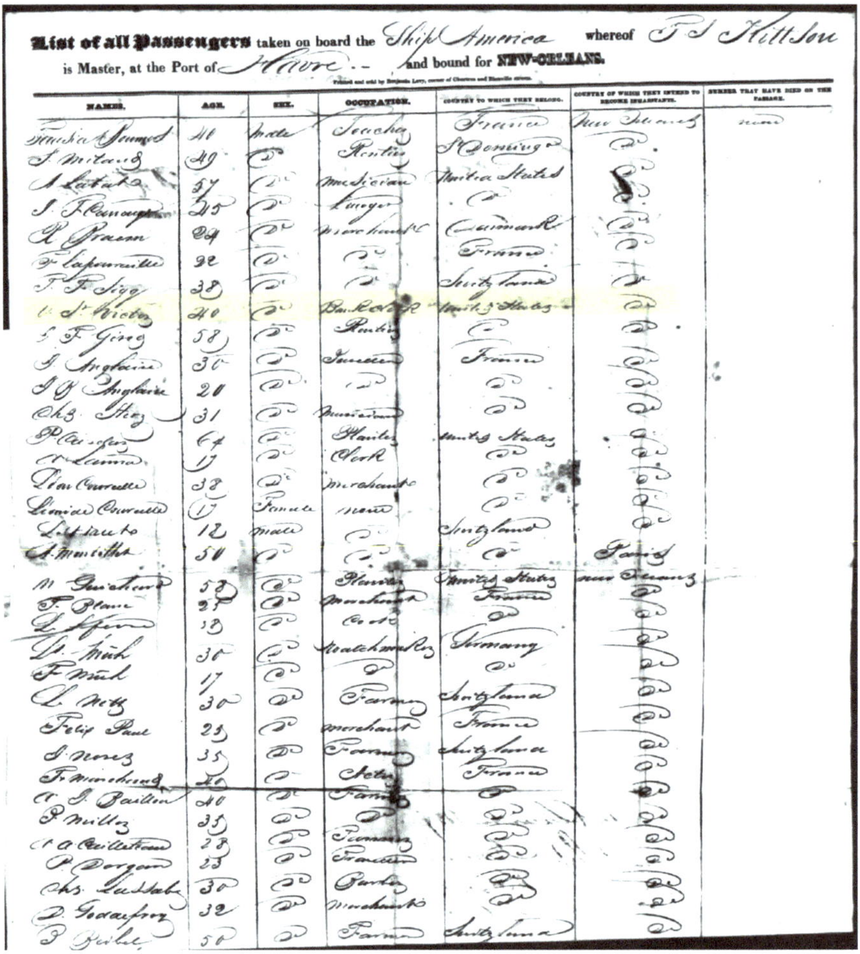

List of all Passengers taken on board the *Ship America* whereof *T J Kittson*
is Master, at the Port of *Havre*.— and bound for **NEW-ORLEANS.**

Printed and sold by Benjamin Levy, corner of Chartres and Bienville streets.

NAMES.	AGE.	SEX.	OCCUPATION.	COUNTRY TO WHICH THEY BELONG.	COUNTRY OF WHICH THEY INTEND TO BECOME INHABITANTS.	NUMBER THAT HAVE DIED ON THE PASSAGE.

Ship's Manifest on Braëm's Voyage

There had been a strong gale from the southwest on the day before our departure and the sea was heavy. It was, therefore, not long before many faces paled and mine was among the number. In spite of the assurances of the pilot, the wind was not from the northwest, but blew directly from the west, so we had to tack right from the beginning, and in the first days, only few were brave enough to eat at the table. Already on the third day, I appeared, and I did not vacate my place at meals for the rest of the journey, although I must admit that I did not always feel equally well, though never better than after a good meal. In this connection, I must further add that the captain had hired a French cook for the benefit of the cabin passengers alone.

Most difficult of all was to pass the time in a pleasant way when we had stormy and rainy days. Some passengers had brought quite a number of books, and I derived some gain and pleasure from reading these, but continuous reading tires even the best, and as for writing, there was forever too much movement of the ship, apart from the fact that one then had to stay down in the cabin, which became intolerable after a while. We then took to playing cards, and I lost money, so it was not one of my happiest inspirations. It is natural that among so many passengers one finds several educated people who can contribute a great deal to the general entertainment, and many hours were also, in fact, spent in such a very pleasant way.

Several previously wealthy planters from Santo Domingo — who had fled to Cuba after the massacre of the whites, and then, after further persecutions there, had continued on to New Orleans and Louisiana — were among our company and their descriptions of their sufferings could not but stir us. However, how much reason they believe they have to detest the blacks and how little esteem this race may deserve, one cannot possibly deny that the expulsion of the whites and the partial annihilation of them are natural results of the whites' own actions and perhaps a retribution for the atrocities of their forefathers against the natives, who were completely exterminated at the time of the first conquest of the island. The mutiny now was caused by the extraordinary declaration of the French government that emancipated all Negroes, who then soon thanked the whites and their mother country by instigating the most atrocious slaughter of humans to finally completely free themselves from the yoke. But sad it is that this island, the richest and most beautiful of all the Antilles, has fallen into such hands and already been changed from extraordinary richness to an equally high degree of poverty.

One of our traveling companions could especially be thanked for helping us to pass the time pleasantly, that is, if one preferred to listen rather than talk, because he spoke enough for all of us when he was not seasick, which happened to him frequently. But I must admit that sometimes we had enough of it, especially when his target was the poor captain, who could not make the slightest change in the sails before the aforementioned — and several others — held a long oration over the lack of wisdom of his move. But worse blame he got when these gentlemen, in their divine wisdom, that one sail or other ought to be adjusted and this did not happen. It was luck that our captain did not understand French; otherwise, it would not all have been so quiet on board. The above-mentioned passenger wished perhaps to show us that he was not a lawyer for nothing and that he had to practice his skill in order not to forget it all on this voyage. He was really a man of knowledge and blessed with a remarkable memory, which continually provided information for us, or so at least we all felt. Apart from him we had another splendid "navigator" on board — the one who really gave our lawyer ammunition for his attacks on the captain. He was an old musician who has a business with musical instruments in New Orleans, where he gives concerts in the winter with his daughters, of whom one is the pupil of Paër and said to be both talented and beautiful. The best about the old man was that he never came on deck except in sunshine and gentle rain. If the weather was less good he never came further than the stairs from where he cast a glance aloft with his head tilted to one side, completely like a hen that sees a hawk in the air, but in this quick glance he discovered so many faults in the setting of the sails that he had enough to complain about for the rest of the day. He was, therefore, rewarded the title "Admiral" and one day he found under his table napkin a large "compass of honor" made of pinewood and with a suitable inscription — and he was, namely, forever making measurements in the chart.

It was natural that so many French people could not be together for long without making up riddles, charades and calembourgs [a word game based on homonyms—*transl.*], some good, some mediocre, but as most of them were improvised we had great fun many an evening. Among the charades, I remember one which I alone guessed, although it was by no means difficult but very true: *mon premier se trouve au milieu de Paris — vous etes enchanté, quant une belle vous dit mon second et mon entier brille parmi les fleurs.* But apart from that I must confess that I was by no means the best at guessing. I must write down one more *jeu de mots,* which we were told and which at its time was very popular in Paris.

Napoleon had sent Maréchal [Jean-Mathieu-Philibert] Serrurier to Constantinople, where Sultan Selim reigned in those days, but the sultan died before the maréchal arrived. One said of that event: *"L'Empereur a envoyé le serrurie rà Constantinople pour raccomoder la Porte, mais quand il y est arrivé il n'a plus trouvé ses limes (Selim)."*

If I could remember everything this book would not suffice, but if I should only select what is worthy of being remembered, a few pages would be sufficient. But it is so that even *des betises* are amusing when one is nearly killed by monotony and heat, and remarks which at a party perhaps would be regarded as insignificant and flat were received here at sea with indulgence, yes, even with interest.

The English Channel is dangerous water when the wind is contrary, especially if it comes from the southwest, which it often does for months, and we have in Le Havre many times seen examples of ships which have tacked outside for three full weeks and then had to return. To our great luck we were not so unfortunate, but were free after eight hard days, but it meant that after these eight days we still had the annoyance of seeing the English coast right opposite Le Havre — a distance that can be covered in less than eighteen hours. The fairer wind we now got was, however, so weak that it took us another four days to clear the Channel; the wind did increase then and brought us in a few days down towards the Azores, but then it turned again to our disadvantage, and we had to pass through the group of islands instead of going east or south round the islands, which would have brought us more quickly into the trade wind.

We first caught sight of Graciosa, and later of Flores, but they were both so far away that it required good eyesight to distinguish them from the clouds. The temperature was already changing, and it got warmer and warmer for each day we got closer to the equator. We would have liked to see Terceira [in 1828-32 Terceira was the scene of heavy battles between the Portuguese strongmen, Koupa, Dom Miguel and Dom Pedro]. This had made it well known, and I must admit that I eagerly looked forward to seeing some Miguelian cruisers. However, it was probably fortunate for us that we did not meet any, and several of the passengers got worried looks on their faces at the sight of a small ketch which passed us at some distance. I must admit that I did nothing to lessen their fears. The theory of those more knowledgeable that we would have difficulty locating the trade wind at our present course was too soon found to be correct, and for two weeks we cruised southward, until finally, on November 12, we got a tailwind so strong that for two weeks we went no less than twenty-four Danish miles per watch [one Danish mile = 4.68 statute miles]. The ocean, however, was rougher than I had expected it would be under a trade wind, and every day we had rain-showers. The sky was a wonderful blue, but never without clouds, and every day we saw the most beautiful rainbows I have ever seen.

The rough seas impeded our fishing considerably, and down by the West Indies we first caught a dolphin on a line which had been in the water for more than a week. I do not believe that there is a more beautiful fish as far as colors go — it is about the size of our cod, from the smallest to the biggest. Its body is actually yellowish gray, and its large dorsal fin is light green, but these colors keep changing, and just before it dies they change from red to yellow and black and blue. Its meat is dry but tasty. It is the main enemy of the flying fish, and it is in order to escape its pursuit, that they fly above the water often several steps above the surface. Sometimes it even came as high as the railing of the ship, and we often got some of them on board. They are very similar to our herring in shape and color, only the head is different, and the fins as well as the sides [of which there are four — fins, that is — two smaller ones closer to the tail] — which are unevenly longer.

We also saw many whales, but only few large ones, as well as armies of porpoises that rose above the ocean's surface. We did not see any sharks, which is very strange. Only near the coast of St. Domingo did we catch two small ones on our lines. The mate let them go immediately since they had an unpleasant odor. The passengers were very upset about this, since he did not even let us have a look at them.

It is not strange that the continual conversations and expressed annoyances over the long voyage and the various opinions regarding the time of our arrival were occasions for wagers. Thus, there were, besides a lot of cigars, one on no less than 5,000 piaster [Spanish coin] whether we would reach the mouth of the Mississippi before December 2. This bet was later canceled, and there were several who thought that it had not been a serious bet. I cannot share this opinion, since I was alone in the cabin when the written conditions were made and there was nothing that pointed toward a joke. I would sooner believe that the loser (who was the least wealthy) had asked the winner to declare that the bet had been called off to avoid any gossip.

One of those gentlemen had his daughter along, the only lady aboard, although she was no beauty, neither in Norwegian nor in Danish, and we had very little interest in her. She was one of those poor animals who always laugh when you talk to them. Her visit to Paris had not been an improvement — her brain did not become any bigger from it. I will admit that this *enchantillon* of the New Orleans ladies did not give me the most favorable notion of the rest of them, until I was told that she was *une fille de couleur* who, like her siblings, did not get to go to the better parties. Her father, like so many here in the colonies, had chosen to live with a woman rather than getting married, and thus had several children who, no matter how well-bred the father was, had to share the fate of the mother, on whom there was less disgrace because she has lived with a man without being married to him than because her blood is not pure.

This prejudice is so strong that one rarely finds white men who will marry such girls, while many have no scruples about living with them, or with one their entire life, and have several children without caring about their fate, especially the daughters, who can only face adversity as long as they live in the colonies. Considering this, it was truly strange to observe the attention and care our traveling companion showed toward his daughter at all times. A young lover would not have been able to do better.

The heat, which could already be felt at the degree of altitude with Portugal, became difficult to endure as soon as we came under the trade wind. It was thus hardly possible to sleep in our cabins because of the heat, and several of us sought refuge on the deck. The canvas, which was left up during the night, sheltered us from the light showers but the heavier ones forced us to rush back inside. This was worse than if we had remained in our berths. Nor was the heavy rocking of the ship exactly very pleasant, especially for the ones who were sleeping on benches, since they occasionally had the unpleasant experience of falling off. In spite of being thoroughly lashed in, I received a few bumps that would hurt for several days. As we got closer to San Domingo and down into the tropics, the seas got calmer and the nights became the most beautiful one could imagine. It seemed especially strange to me to be forced to sleep under open sky at the beginning of December, due to the hot weather, since in the middle of April I had crossed the ice for over seven miles.

On November 27, we sighted the northeast coast of Santo Domingo, and I had the honor of being the first to espy the land. It was very high and seemed almost black. We got within 4 to 5 miles of the coast and through binoculars we were able to distinguish mountains and forests. On this side the island is very thinly populated, but we did see smoke rising from three different locations on the beach.

Due to calm weather, we were forced to spend five days along the coast of this wonderful island, and I have never experienced a more perfect nature anywhere. It spread its riches, and the nights, illuminated by the waxing moon and the most glittering stars on the blue southern sky, were enchanting. A soft wind, just refreshing the air, filled the sails just enough to flap against the mast, and I went to sleep every night with the hope that we were not to leave this area soon, which made me forget the reality of soon having to make my decision. Although these Santo Domingo nights were beautiful, they were overshadowed by the mornings that relieved them, when the sun rose in a splendor to which I have never seen the like, while the clouds, which made a circle in the horizon, formed the most wonderful shapes with the rising sun, shapes like animals and then humans in the most amazing positions. It was impossible to imagine a more beautiful sky, although it was not only the eye which could enjoy the wonderful morning air, but it also brought a beautiful scent of flowers, and it all brought me great enjoyment, which will be difficult to forget. The high land also brought a striking view, namely, the clouds soaring at the top of the mountains. For one who has never witnessed such natural phenomena, it leaves a great impression.

At the entrance to the former Cape Français, which in the time of the French was a very wealthy city of over 50,000 inhabitants, we caught sight of two warships that appeared to be corvettes. They were cruising close to the shore. At sunset one came so close to us that we could hear the waves at its bow, and the commands shouted on board. However, it was already so dark that we were unable to determine its strength or its flag, and the next morning it was almost out of sight. My heart was beating at the thought that it could possibly be our *Diana*. The island of Tortuga [Tortoises], which we passed near Santo Domingo, was at one time a plantation and its owners were very wealthy. It is now almost deserted. The Negroes did not work hard enough to earn their daily bread, and were as lazy as the Cubans. These wonderful islands with the most beautiful climate in such hands! It is hard to fathom.

On December 2, the wind improved, and we made better time on that day than on the previous five days together. We saw Cabo Maisi, Cuba's most easterly point, in the distance, and closed in on the southeast part of the island at a speed of six to seven miles. We were to go south of it, since the captain was unfamiliar with the potentially more dangerous coast of the Bahamas. We came within a few miles of the high coast, which appeared green and to be very fertile; however, it appeared to be lightly populated and overgrown with brush.

The French immigrants from Santo Domingo who were aboard assured us that if the Spaniards had not most shamefully broken their word by exiling them when they sought refuge on the island and had already bought plantations and farms there, this part of Cuba would by now be far better cultivated and fertile than the western part, which in spite of the laziness of the Spaniards produces such large amounts of coffee, sugar, tobacco, etc. There is no doubt that the more industrious French would have introduced a big improvement.

The sun set before we got to a point on the ocean where, in clear weather, we would be able to see the three coasts of Cuba, Santo Domingo and Jamaica at the same time. The next morning, we were able to see only the first and the last of these islands in the distance. We were able to see Jamaica the entire day, and since the wind was fair we came already the next morning close to the south of the Grand Caiman, where we could distinguish houses and trees, and, of these, the experts were able to distinguish between the various sorts. I say experts, since regarding plantains, palms, coconut trees and others that thrive in this wonderful climate, I had but little knowledge. The Grand and Small Caimans are two smaller islands which, as well as Jamaica, belong to England.

Our course, which this far had been West, with a more or less southern direction, changed to NW after we had passed the Caimans, in order to get around Cabo San Antonio on Cuba, after which we went straight North. Thus, the most southerly I got so far was 18° degrees, 20 minutes; that is, a latitude which has the sun in zenith during the summer and which yields the richest and most beautiful produce on earth. It was very interesting to me to notice at this southern latitude that the celestial bodies changed positions. Just as the Pole star went closer to the horizon, new stars appeared on the southern horizon, and the proud Big Dipper, which both summer and winter is so resplendent in the sky to us, at times completely disappeared beneath the horizon, while the "Giant" rose higher and higher, so that its shoulders were almost above my head. Since I had anticipated a great part of the southern sky, I had purchased in Le Havre "*un Manuel d'Astronomie*," but unfortunately, I only found a map of the northern celestial map in it, and thus became no wiser.

When we got near to the Mexican coast, the air was very heavy, with a strong and fair wind, so we did not get any view of the Cuban coast. This could have been our luck, since at the western approach to the island, Cabo San Antonio, is a well-known pirates' nest, which the Spaniards not only tolerate, but protect. One of our fellow passengers had been robbed by them a few years earlier, and his tale did not make any of us wish to make their acquaintance. However, I believe that one would have defended himself, if they had come aboard, although the ship had neither cannons nor rifles. At least, there were many who appeared to have enough courage now, but if they would have it then, is a different question.

The Gulf of Mexico, which everyone agreed could be very bad, and sometimes worse than the ocean, received us only dark and rough, but later became as calm as one could wish. The wind came more from the north, and soon formed only a few lines in the sail, and we could change our course. On this occasion, our captain, about whose capabilities the super-smart passengers had much to say, showed us that he knew what he was doing. Although the wind had driven us far to the west and there were heavy currents in the gulf, and the entrance to the Mississippi is very difficult to approach, the first land we sighted was the mouth of the river. Our musician wanted to bet his French horn that we were closer to the Mexican coast than Louisiana, and another gentleman on board, who had been a French naval officer, bet five hundred cigars against one that we had drifted at least fifty miles toward the west and would not reach the river mouth without changing course or tack. It is true that our captain did not understand how to judge the distance, and both he and the first mate assured me that it was a science that had not yet been mastered. I apologized for my ignorance; otherwise it would have been a joy for me to take them in.

It is indeed strange that one has the opinion that the Americans are so knowledgeable about the sea, and that it is actually by luck or natural ability that they understand to defend their name. It is a fact that neither skippers nor their first mates are required to pass any kind of examination and that any ship-owner can give the command of his ship to a farm boy if he desires. Nonetheless, and this is strange, any American sailor is considered to have much better knowledge and ability than the French, who among all nations are the ones who are subject to the most strict testing of their overall knowledge. The reason may lie in the well-known aptitude of the Americans and English for sailing, which is visibly lacking in the French.

Mississippi, one of the greatest rivers on earth, and taking into consideration its enormous navigable length, the many other big rivers which flow into it, the wealth of the land that it and its numerous tributaries protect, and the merchandise it alone provides transportation for, it is probably one of the most important of all rivers.

Mississippi makes its presence known in many ways long before one sees the coasts of the country through whose mighty stretches it flows. However, none of these methods gives a pleasant impression to the traveler. The first thing one notices is an off-shore current, and ships always seek to avoid the lanes in the ocean which mark the flow of that current on the maps. The most prominent and most unpleasant indications of the proximity of the river is a heavy cold fog, which always hangs over the mouth of the river and many times reaches far into the ocean. It often makes it difficult to find the mouth of the river.

We were perhaps ten miles from the coast when, in the distance, we saw something dark over the horizon that looked like land, but which the better informed ones assured us was the fog. It was not long before it closed in, accompanied by such a powerful change in the atmosphere that the thermometer in the span of one hour dropped by no less than 24° to 30° F, and forced us, who during the morning had been suffering from the heat, dressed as lightly as possible, to completely change clothes and even put on capes and coats. It was not the fog alone which looked like land, but the flood water.

The flood water, which also can be seen several miles out in the ocean, completely changes the color of the ocean after having undergone several changes in shading (one of the learned Mr. Elm's words, which does not appear to be quite as unfortunate as the others). It would appear clear and soon more or less muddy. The river water can only with the greatest of difficulty and after a long battle, get the clean, clear ocean water to mix with it. This gives me the truest picture of the white and the black races, and of what the consequences of the battle will be. The river water, crystal clear, soft and pleasant when it has undergone a filtration, is the ugliest color in its natural condition. Entire clouds of mud flow in long strips out into the ocean on top of and beside the clear ocean water. It looked as if the water, in a pool had been set in motion with a stick, and it contributes as little as all of the other things one gradually notices, to announce the rich country through which it has flowed.

One will necessarily get a completely different impression at the sight of the mass of wood and trees, in lengths of sixty to eighty feet, drifting with the river and far into the ocean, especially with the knowledge the Europeans have of the value of trees. This is completely different in a country in which the forests are so superfluous that they are set afire in order for man to be able to till the soil. It is certain, however, that if the population had been denser and labor not so scarce, one would hardly, with the great consumption of firewood by the many steamships, which use nothing else, let so many trees flow for hundreds of miles without cutting them up somewhere. Yet labor is so expensive here that in New Orleans, where many make a living by fishing up the driftwood, one must pay more for wood than anywhere I have been in Europe, maybe with the exception of Amsterdam.

On the morning of December 9, after fifty-four days of sailing, we finally sighted the coast of Louisiana, and thus the United States of America. Due to calm weather we were unable to get a pilot on board until the next morning, and I found it incomprehensible that we were close to land before the pilot made an effort to row his dinghy out and get aboard, a negligence caused by the lack of need to compete, since all pilots worked for one master and there were no benefits associated by being the first one aboard. I must admit that this first impression I received of arrangements in the most free and sensible state, and where a half century worth of wonders alone are a credit to freedom and competition, were just as unexpected as they were unpleasant. I am fortunate to be able to add that in other places and on the coasts of the Atlantic Ocean this is not the case, and that the mouth of the Mississippi is completely free of rocks.

Braëm's Passenger Ticket 12.16.1829

Map from Rudolph Braëm's Diary
He underlined each city that he visited
and recorded the population of each city.

New Orleans, Louisana

The Eastern delta where we landed had previously been the main inlet and, for that reason, at much expense and difficulty, a lighthouse has been erected on an insecure base, which consists of only pile-ups that have, with time, become halfway solid piles carried down by the river. Lately, the river delta has less depth, but to the SW there is more water at this time. We thus had to sail there and by the time we cast anchor in the evening, there were 16 other ships, of which 12 were three-masters of the most beautiful construction, as are most of the American ships, and most of those were aground, partly outside and partly in the mouth of the river. Only high tide would be able to get them off, and the ships did not suffer any damage while stuck in the mud.

The entire coast with five inlets here is the saddest sight one can imagine, and this more so after one comes from coasts such as Cuba and Santo Domingo. One can hardly see any land due to the reeds, which stretch like bushes halfway under water all the way, and since at high tide the entire delta formed by the river is thus under water, it is natural that there have been no thoughts of populating and less of tilling it. A good eye can thus only distinguish a few small shacks for the pilots among the reeds. As far as one can see inland, there is only muddy water and reeds and no hint of trees or hills, while the ears can enjoy the eternal sounds of pelicans and other sea birds, while they soar in big flocks over the sea and bog. That is the way Louisiana announces itself, one of the most fertile countries, and one which will become one of the most important as time passes. The beautiful fleet of which we became part was a striking contrast to the poor and wild nature, the terrible melancholic appearance of which I cannot find words to express.

I feel that a few remarks about the former Louisiana are called for before I step ashore — because the present is only a very small part of it. Not until the end of the 17th Century was the mighty Mississippi River visited by Europeans. It was the French who, at the time, were masters over all of Canada, which now belongs to the English. The radical plan of the first explorers was to take possession of all the land from the great lakes south of Canada, and along the Ohio and Mississippi rivers to the Mexican Gulf. All of this was covered with impenetrable forests and populated by wild tribes. The French thus wanted to prevent the English, who at the time were occupying the coast, from moving farther to the west, and to divide the Mississippi with them. The French government could only second the plan. However, the lack of knowledge about the conditions of the country and their importance as far as products goes forced them to establish a company, which ended up, like so many later ones, in ruining itself and costing the state in taxes. At the beginning of the previous century, they founded the city of New Orleans, named after the then French regent, the Duke of Orleans, and Louisiana after Louis XIV. A city which needed a free and liberal government as a member of the most free and happy state on earth in order to elevate itself to what it already is, and after all fairness will become one of the first commercial cities on earth.

This country, to which France thus made claim — naturally without the slightest consideration for the rights of the natives — stretches from 29° to ca. 47° northern latitude and in width, from the Mississippi River to the Pacific Ocean, a country about which they did not have the slightest knowledge. It is only during the later years that the government of the United States has let its almost impenetrable forests and enormous mountain regions become travel worthy. A bigger burden than advantage for the country, Louis XV in

1763 ceded it all to Spain by a family treaty, to which it probably was a bigger problem. Without argument the Spanish government thus honored France's claim to the land after the French revolution brought down Louis XV's right to cede it by a family treaty just like a piece of furniture, and a new transfer took place against the relinquishing of some demands which France thought they had against Spain.

That is the way things were when Napoleon as First Consul took over the government and changed the country's pitiful internal and external condition to the way we have known it. He immediately remarked on the impossibility of holding on to such a colony, of which the revolutionary wars had hindered the French in again taking possession. Rather than let the English take it for nothing, he decided to suggest ceding it to the United States, which, just at that time, had an ambassador in Paris to work out a treaty for free shipping on the Mississippi river and to receive the city of New Orleans located on the left bank of the river. Instead of this, the unexpected offer was made to the negotiators to cede the entire land area to which France had claim, which, in area, exceeded all of the United States together, for a sum of money. Since it should be obvious to anybody of what incalculable importance the possession of such land had to be to the American Free State, they accepted the offer of 80 million francs, a sum which Napoleon needed badly. In this manner, this land, which is larger than France, Spain and Portugal combined, got a free government, a country under the most beautiful heavens and with the most fertile soil.

At dawn on the following morning, December 11, that is, about 5:30 a.m., we sighted two steamships that had towed ships down and were going around to those who were anchored up in order to offer their services. These steamboats had a strange appearance, resembling floating houses since their cabin and machinery were located on the deck. The first one had two stories, but since the boat is not very large there were only four windows on each side. In the front were two chimneys exactly alike. Across and between the two, a little aft and under a roof, was the helmsman.

Our captain agreed with him to have him tow us in for the sum of 250 piaster, and he tied us to his side, then tied another brig to the other side, and thus we advanced without worrying about current or wind. However, as long as we were in the river mouth, the view was the same: muddy river water, reeds and here and there some willow trees. There was no change until the following morning, and it was not unpleasant. When I got up on the deck, I saw that we were surrounded by forest, which reached clear down to the water and appeared to be impenetrable. The river bed was so straight that it looked more like a wide channel, while the forest, or rather the dense scrub, for a long time remained without noticeable openings. The river banks were here, as everywhere else, filled with tree trunks, which had drifted down and lay in the most varied and irregular positions, adding much to the striking wilderness all around. Just as the reeds at the mouth teemed with crocodiles and all kinds of seabirds, the bushes along the river were full of all kinds of snakes, among these were the most dangerous. The crocodiles, alligators, do not attack people unless they are provoked or very hungry. We did not see any, since they are hibernating at this time of the year. During the night we passed Fort Jackson, a fortification which guards the river and is completely unassailable. Since it was built, at great expense and difficulty, in an almost bottomless morass, no enemy has been able to get near it from the land side, and the shallow depths of the river mouth prevent any big warships from coming into the river and thus, from attacking it.

Only about eight miles from the mouth of the river and ca. 10 miles from the city, they have started to establish plantations and clear the forest. Nothing can give a more clear impression of the houses of the natives in a newly tilled land than these first plantations that we passed. On all sides were forests in their natural wildness, even along the river bank there was a thin row of all kinds of trees through which one could see a rather large wooden cabin in the middle of a couple of acres of land that had been cleared but was full of stumps. Among these had been planted corn and rice, of which some was still standing.

The house or cabin, with a protruding roof with supports, had openings but no windows, and through these peeped black and brown faces. The women were clothed in dresses with short sleeves and no belts, the men were in shirtsleeves, and the children, who ran around among donkeys, pigs and poultry in just shirts, all were without footwear. The farther we went, the more civilized it appeared to be, and, as soon as we got to the sugar plantations, every moment was a joy to the eye, with magnificent residences with gardens full of fruit-bearing orange trees and with steam engines in full swing squeezing sugar from the sugarcanes. The slaves usually live behind the residence in small cabins, each equipped for one family and with a small garden. Several new plantations had these cabins beautifully painted, and in numbers so large that it looked like a regular village.

Of the same width as the river is short, before it divides into its five or six mouths, it almost remains — that is, sometimes a little wider and sometimes a little narrower – for several hundred miles (I am still talking about Danish miles) inland. And its depth, which according to the maps, is barely 12 to 15 feet, is on the whole stretch so enormous that it cannot be determined and is commonly from 30 to 50 fathoms. It is thus incomprehensible that the miserable levees along both banks do not break down more often, since the river is extremely narrow in relation to its depth. I estimate it to be no more than 100 to 150 fathoms wide.

The distance from the mouth of the river to New Orleans is about 18 miles, a distance the steamships usually cover in twelve hours while towing ships down and from twenty-four to twenty-eight hours going up. However, our ship was not of the best, and besides ours and the brig they took in tow a ketch that was lying tied to a tree trunk in the river. Although the wind was strong enough that we at times pulled the steamship, it took us thirty-four hours to reach the city. We did not get there until about nine o'clock and thus did not have the pleasure of gradually seeing our destination.

The sugar plantations of one of our fellow travelers were located a couple of miles down from the city. The owner saw lights and went to the ship's railing when we were just even with it and gave a strong whistle through his fingers. The sound had no more than reached land before there were shouts: "*v'la le vieux maitre, v'la le vieux maitre!*" The Negroes knew his signal and came running down to the river bank, welcomed their master, and told him that everything was well. He ordered them to send his carriage to the harbor.

There were many ships in the river at the city, and we were placed in the fourth line. From the innermost ship, there is a bridge formed by two planks resting on the ship. There is no wharf for the ships to be tied to, but the river is so deep that these bridges are seldom more than 40 feet long. It is still inconvenient for the innermost ship that the others must unload and load across them. This could be prevented by using barges, but it would increase the cost considerably, and they could not always be used due to the strong current.

Besides the great comfort after a long voyage of knowing that one is getting close to one's destination this also brings out, in the company of many passengers, another interest. The conversation becomes livelier, with many subjects of which acquaintances in the country have not previously thought of becoming materials for entertaining comments. Thus, the last days, instead of being considered emptied of entertainment, are usually the most enjoyable. That which also is enjoyable on the final day, is the total change taking place in the exterior of the travelers. While on board everyone is satisfied to wear old clothes, and very few are particular in how they dress. As we get closer to our destination, a complete transformation takes place, with the shabbiest looking ones becoming the greatest "*petit maitre*" [fop]. Since most of my fellow travelers came from Paris, one could almost, the way they were transformed, consider each one a model for the latest fashion.

Just to go ashore one does not dress in everyday clothing, but for people to be more striking, they dress in their best for the occasion, and the altered facial expressions must not be forgotten, either. Everyone is easygoing and content, and only the wrinkles of old age are not eradicated.

My first impression of New Orleans was not the most pleasant. I did not see much in the evening, but early the next morning, on a walk along the river, where the ships were on one side of me and houses and shops on the other, I did not find it to be the way I had expected. The entire stretch I walked consisted of small, wretched and poorly maintained buildings, and each of them, without exception, had a shop. Even the walls of an entire block of burned buildings had been changed into stores without doing any other improvements other than making sure they were enclosed. Later on, I heard that an old scoundrel who everyone, without exception, assured me deserved the gallows several times over, had bought these lots for 80,000 piaster in order to have the pleasure of annoying the public by leaving it that way. Higher up the street became more beautiful, since this is where the American part of the city begins. It is new and has three- and four-story houses, while the French part, especially at some distance from the center, only consists of one-story houses.

What amused me the most on my first walk, were the Negroes, who stood in groups on the corners. Sometimes they spoke English and, at other times, Creole French. The languages of two nations, which in so many respects are very different, and which only in this place on earth are shared by the inhabitants and even by the government, which functions in both languages. But this is all they have in common. Although neither English nor French, but American, both families maintain in large part their original prejudices and almost hatred to each other. This is expressed at any opportunity in public as well as in private, and while many young Creoles [racially mixed children born in the colonies to French parents] determine it to be an honor to forget their French in favor of English, it will be centuries before a complete merger takes place, if it is even possible.

The city is built in a semi-circle around a bend in the river and is completely regular. The streets are a convenient width, and all have sidewalks made of tiles or brick. However, since Louisiana by nature does not have any boulders, large or small, and all paving stones must be brought in from hundreds of miles away, and often come from Europe as ballast, it is not as strange as intolerant foreigners find it that most of the streets are unsuitable for paving. Since the soil is extremely rich, it is adversely affected by even the least amount of rain. There is even the story that a few years ago a horse and fully loaded wagon disappeared in the middle of the street, and they even had to pay a piaster to have a bale of cotton brought out to the ship. Now all the streets with the heaviest traffic — and there are many of them — are paved. Yet since the ground is so loose and the paving stones very ineffectual, one can soon see that this is of little advantage for the finances of the city.

I had room and board in a French house, which was recommended to me by one of my fellow passengers at a cost of forty-five piaster per month. Since the rent is extremely high and the inns during the four dangerous months earn nothing, they take advantage of this any way they can, and, during the other time, for instance, place several beds in a room in order to accommodate more travelers. Since I did not dream that this was the purpose of the other bed in my room, I was surprised in the evening when I found there was a stranger in it, without having heard a word about it. When I, on the following day, protested vehemently, I received the simple answer: that is the custom in this country. A Dutchman would have thought: "*Lands wys, lands eer*" [country's way, country's honor] — a proverb they always used to defend much of their foolishness — and would have accepted it. I was less phlegmatic and brought the matter so far that the bed was removed and I became sole master of my room.

They say that inland one is happy if one is able to find lodging in the company of five others in the same room.

I was very satisfied with the board, and the company I found there — ten–twelve young English and Americans and some American families — was very pleasant. The food and drink were French, but the table service was quite English or American, with the entire meal being served together and individuals taking what they like the best without worrying about any order or their fellow diners. The result is that one must be fast if one does not want to eat just leftovers, and the meal is thus quickly finished. The occupations of the Americans — since very few of them are members of the community — make this rush a natural thing. But for the one who has not adjusted his eating habits to this, it is far from pleasant. There is no servant class, just slaves, namely the Negroes, who serve at the table, and there are ten of them, where in Europe we have at the most two. It was an unpleasant sight at first, before you get used to the terrible slavery. After a while, it dissipates just as everything else, although I am convinced that the prediction by my fellow travelers that after being in New Orleans for a month, my attitude in that respect would change and be more like theirs, will never come true.

The conversation at the table is practically all in English. Although several of the Americans and English have chosen this house in order to practice their French everyone understands English well enough that a different language is not necessary. If one can manage in one's mother tongue even the best principles are seldom able to suspend it. Since I needed to practice English more than French, this was most welcome to me, and I soon became closely acquainted with an Englishman and an American who roomed together, and, in the company of them and some of their friends, I have spent many pleasant evenings. Such a refuge is necessary here, where everyone only thinks about making money while sacrificing almost all forms of social pleasures. Thus, there is only one family as "*recoit*" [receiver] as in France, and there is very seldom an invitation to a soiree, which is noticeable among the many originally French families, who in all other respects go according to their land of origin. There is not even a club here, and thus the evenings are killers to strangers who do not feel like wasting piaster every night on comedy. It is, therefore, not strange that the residents of New Orleans do not find more time for reading than for other diversions, and that there are no reading organizations, although many have been started. A new one will be started next January, but it is not predicted that it will fare better, and I expect to be able to talk more about that later.

The official amusements here consist of a French and an English theater and many balls. Maybe one could add to this several gambling houses, although the majority of their visitors are hardly of that opinion when they leave them. The French actors are all from France and are numerous and talented enough to present anything from the lowest farce to the grandest opera and drama and, all in all, present as good an ensemble as the best provincial theaters in France. Since the French-speaking and fair sex is numerous and from wealthy — in Europe one would say rich — families, the rare phenomenon exists that a theater manager can survive in spite of the enormous cost of salaries for up to 40 persons, their travel expenses from France and subsistence expenses at a location that is probably the most expensive on earth. The cost of admission is also in accordance to that, and a gentleman "*en peu comme il faut*" cannot go to a place that costs less than 1½ piaster [three Rbd Silver]. As far as I am concerned, I must admit that at that price I find very little diversion in comedies and thus, go there very seldom. On the other hand, I go to the American or English theaters more often, where the cost is one piaster, especially since there sometimes are some quite good actors from up north. I am no fan of

English comedies in general, where at the expense of the natural they only aim for effect, which mainly consist of jokes of the worst kind as in… [sic].

When one is used to the French vaudevilles filled with jokes and…[sic] and decent fun, these immense embarrassments fall flat. It is thus also less for the fun in the plays that I watch the performances than to take advantage of the language, which here is plenty unrestrained. The plays cease during the bad season, when the terrible heat would make both performance and attendance impossible. The French cast spends that time in the northern cities of New York, Boston and Philadelphia — a journey of several hundred miles, for which only God knows where the manager finds the money to pay. But it is a condition under which he would not keep a single person in a place where, on the average, nine out of ten foreigners die during the dangerous time of the year.

It is only since New Orleans has become such an important commercial town and many foreigners have arrived that yellow fever has been known here, since it has only killed foreigners. The strangest part is that it has only hit foreigners who stay in the city itself — one mile away, they could be out of danger. It is thus incomprehensible that so many will expose themselves to the worst when, at a low cost, they could spend the four months when no business is transacted in the countryside. But most of the ones coming here to stay are knights of fortune, who only value life to the extent it provides pleasures, and, since they seldom know others than the ones money can buy, they forget their duties to family, friends and themselves by risking a life over which they are not masters. We all know, however, how difficult it is to judge the feelings of others, and I must admit that my eloquence against such self-sacrifice was badly hurt when I was told that even a reformed priest, a young kindly man who had arrived from France a few years ago as the first French Protestant pastor in New Orleans, last year had become the victim of his stubbornness at not wanting to leave the city, as he had done for two summers. Also, he wanted to try his luck, and that was only possible by continuing a school which he had started. That which seduces these people to stay after they have spent some time in the city, is that the fever does not strike every year, and by hitting a couple of good summers one can sometimes get acclimatized to it.

The arrival of many half-naked Spaniards from Mexico caused the large number of fatalities last summer, and it is usually after a few good years in which the foreigners have built up their confidence that an illness comes which takes almost all of them out. Without this plague, New Orleans, which had already attained great importance, would soon have become the first city in the union. It was not only foreigners who were considered strangers, but anyone from the northern states, which during the good season makes up half of the population and almost all of whom leave the city during the summer. Business also ceases completely, and instead of a couple of hundred ships coming to the city at one time, there are sometimes only three. Legal proceedings also come to a complete stop, for those who know the city during the busy season and who themselves are business people neither yellow fever nor killing heat is necessary to make staying there intolerable during the bad months. I mentioned earlier that a mile away from here there was no danger for a stranger. This is probably correct, since at a mile's distance one is in the country. But if one goes farther away and gets to the first cities upriver, it again becomes unhealthy, which proves that the sickness is only caused by the contact of the air with emanations of the masses, and in no way by the air alone. They are also convinced that the yellow fever is not contagious, and yet trade and shipping in Europe are plagued by continual quarantines.

While talking about mortality rates and death, I want to use the occasion to comment on this city's strange cemetery, since I have had nothing to do with these sad objects for a long time. The outer, fertile banks of the Mississippi are for hundreds of miles so low that where they are tilled dikes are needed to protect the plantations against flooding of the river.

This takes place anywhere the axe and spade of the agriculturist have not yet made their way to a superfluous yield from the rich soil. The levees alone do not keep the soil behind it from getting wet, and in many places to such a high degree that a hole no deeper than through the sod is instantly filled with water as soon as it is dug, a condition which makes the tilling of the soil very difficult. New Orleans is built on such soil and is, therefore, halfway under water, and the same is the case behind the city where the cemetery is located. This creates a strange sight. In order to avoid the repulsiveness of drowning the bodies, which the poor people must suffer, since no matter how shallow the grave is, it is immediately filled with water, which makes it necessary to drill holes in the casket so it can sink. To avoid this, a wall has been erected which is eight to ten feet high and almost eight feet thick, with three levels with holes in which the caskets are placed, and then they are bricked up. On the outside at the end is most often a marble slab with the name of the person buried there. Besides these, there are many individual and family grave plots, all of brick above ground and usually with a fence around and a few bushes and flowers like at our cemeteries. By reading the inscriptions, I could only shiver at seeing the many foreigners who have died during the summer months and thus, no doubt from the yellow fever. Emanations from this cemetery are sometimes intolerable during the heat of summer and perhaps contribute to the fact that there are so many victims of the yellow fever here.

Yet another division between the original French and English families than the ones mentioned is religion. Though nothing but liberals in such a liberal country, the first ones remain Catholic, while, as known, the great majority of Americans are Protestants and very active in their numerous sects. The Catholics have two churches, the cathedral and a chapel in the former monastery. The Americans have already built five larger and smaller ones, of which two are Reformed, one Episcopalian, one Methodist and one Anabaptist. One of the Reformed is only half finished due to lack of money, and that is the way it often goes with the enterprising Americans, who do not always consider their strength before they start their work. The church is specifically for seamen and of a poor style, which most of the official American buildings here are. It is under the roof and up very high from the ground to enable them to rent the lower level to grocers and other merchants.

In my opinion, this style is just too commercial, and it is strange that on this occasion they have not used the common means of raising money, namely by authorizing a lottery. There are many such entrepreneurs in the union, who offer money for public works in return for being authorized to have a lottery, which can be continued until they have raised enough money plus a 30 percent profit. In this manner the French Protestants have been able to build a church, the pastor of which died last summer, as I mentioned earlier. Since this is the way it is done on public projects throughout Louisiana, there are lottery drawings at least two times every week. The coupons are arranged in squares instead of numbers as we do it. Since a whole coupon seldom costs less than four piaster, and thus one-quarter, which is the smallest fraction sold, would cost one piaster, they are less appealing to the laboring class than a number lottery would be. It would, however, probably be better if the wise government of the United States had not found it necessary to permit lotteries, which continually keep duping the people.

The city's surroundings are not very attractive. Along the levee to the south, there are many pleasure places where the evergreen gardens and roses along the fences are a pleasant sight for northerners in December. Those houses are usually built in a uniform style, namely, a long, protruding roof, resting all around on thin wooden pillars. The houses are usually green and the pillars white, very well maintained. The projecting roof protects against the terrible heat from the sun, and all the roofs on the one-story houses in New Orleans are built that way, but do not rest on pillars.

Many of these houses in the city are very pretty, but so modestly arranged as far as space goes that if one goes up two steps from the street, one will be in the living room, which is often very luxuriously furnished. It is thus sometimes necessary to walk across an expensive carpet with dirty boots. It would be a big mistake to think that this was an example of poor hygiene on the part of the inhabitants, a virtue which people from the first families to the poorest Negro to a high degree possess. It is just as rare to see dirty clothing on the native[s] as it is for us to see clean rags on the poor. There are no beggars here, and anyone, who is willing to work earns at least one piaster a day. The climate here does not attract idlers. A well- equipped and large hospital provides plenty of care for the sick.

Right behind the city is the so-called Cypress, a sort of pine forest of almost never-ending wood, which stretches down to an inlet of the ocean for a distance of almost 1½ miles. These trees grow in the bog, and one cannot go through the woods without getting into water to one's waist. They have been mainly cleared here, and a small canal has been dug down to the lake, from which many goods are transported to the city. During the summer months, this is a common evening trip for the "*beau monde,*" who then swim in the lake. A new rail line is planned down to the lake, and that will increase the traffic and probably for some time make this into the only resort for the people from New Orleans.

The weather has been very pleasant this month since my arrival. We have even had a few warm days and a few cool days. On Christmas Eve, we had an oppressive heat, which ended with a terrible thunderstorm and downpour, which here is much heavier than in Europe. The north wind always brings cooler weather this time of the year, and it usually is sudden and violent, so the temperature can drop 10° in half an hour and all window shutters and doors in town rattle in its presence. This sudden change in temperature makes much caution necessary, especially for strangers, although the wind, as mentioned, announces the arrival of the cold in plenty of time that one without risk can change clothes. This wind often brings on hurricanes so violent that ships have been lost in the river and buildings in the plantations have collapsed.

These busy people celebrate only very few holidays, and, this Christmas, I only had the memories of the previous one to keep me happy. It was only by holding an almanac in my hand that it was possible to imagine that it was that time of the year. It's necessary companions seem to be short days, snow and ice, and a warm stove.

January 1830

A very strange woman, whose presence will make this an epoch in the American history, arrived here with the new year. She is the first philosopher who has dared to step out in public and preach against the Christian religion and its teachers. Frances Wright is almost thirty-five years of age, a tall and beautiful woman. Born in England into a very wealthy family, she received a thorough education, but her uncommon curiosity could not be compared to common knowledge. She wanted to know the reason for everything, especially religion, and when her teachers' answers did not satisfy her, she started her own studies and soon thought that she had discovered prejudices and superstitions, where others saw reasons and sound knowledge. She continued on and on, especially through the works of the old philosophers, found common sense in them, contradictions in the Bible, but especially in the speeches of the ones who proclaimed it. She started to express her opinions about freedom, although she was still so young. However, she soon realized that she was unable to reform the world, which she, at the time, maybe did not consider doing. She went to America after first having spent a long period of time in Paris to continue her studies, and thereby spent a good part of her fortune.

Frances Wright
(1795–1852)

Already, while in Paris, she had written a thesis in the style of the old philosophers, in which was included, many sound concepts. She was now beginning to carry out her principles of freedom and equality. It was no wonder that her attention would first fall on the slavery of the southern states, and her thoughts and means [dwelt on] how to alleviate this misery. She, therefore, traveled down to Tennessee, and bought a cotton plantation with about thirty Negroes [and] with the intention of estimating the annual value of their work, and thus allowing them to purchase their freedom by working. By doing this, she hoped to convince other plantation owners of the possibility of abolishing slavery, and that it was to their benefit. Instead of following her example, she received mockery for her efforts. When she saw the impossibility of accomplishing her philanthropic plan in that manner, and her plantation being unprofitable, she decided to give her slaves their freedom and bring them to Haiti. That is the reason she came to New Orleans.

It was during her stay in Cincinnati, an important city in Ohio, a few years ago that she first decided to step forth as a public speaker and as a fighter against prejudice and a solicitor for the spread of useful and positive knowledge and sensible upbringing. The quarrels among the various sects in Cincinnati at the time, which had almost brought on an open feud, was the best occasion for her decision, and, at the same time, brought her many followers. Encouraged by this, she stepped forth in New York, Philadelphia, Boston and other big cities, establishing sects everywhere that opened so-called Halls of Science, where there were lectures every Sunday on useful subjects such as physics, chemistry, mathematics, ethics, etc. Since they considered religion as the most absurd thing in the world, and which has only spread darkness, quarrels and misery, one understands that it forever is excluded from the hall of knowledge. In order to further strengthen her teachings, she has already, for several years, in the company of a very capable man, R. D. Owen, published a weekly magazine, *The Free Enquirer*.

In this a republican education, where all children are equal, and her other basic tenets are developed and the principles of the opposition are fought down. In it, all of the teachings of the Christian religion are tried and developed in the most free manner, which cannot be prevented, since the government of the United States does not interfere in religion, and even a

THE

FREE ENQUIRER.

VOLUME I.

FROM OCTOBER 29, 1828 TO OCTOBER 21, 1829.

JUST OPINIONS ARE THE RESULT OF JUST KNOWLEDGE,—JUST PRACTICE OF JUST OPINIONS.

NEW-YORK:

PRINTED AT THE OFFICE OF THE FREE ENQUIRER.

1829.

Abolitionist Newspaper

Mohammedan has the same rights as a Calvinist in the eye of the highest authorities of the state if he is not lacking citizenship status. Since most of the ones who bear the name "Christian" are no better than Miss Wright, it is not strange that they have had the courage to take the first step and break the ice. Many are seeking in her teachings what they were missing in the other and hang on to it, at least while it is new, but it is strange that almost at the same time, Miss Wright appeared there was a split among the Quakers [perhaps referring to The "great separation" of 1827–28, which began in their Philadelphia Yearly Meeting], the majority of whom abandoned the dogmas and mysteries of Christianity and adopted almost entirely her principles. Such an action by a sect, which was famous for its piety, made a big impression on the entire country and could have important consequences.

On the 4th, she gave her first lecture in the American Theater to a large audience, which probably was there out of curiosity. I must admit that it was something extraordinary seeing a woman appear in public as an advocate for the non-religious and unbelieving, and my heart was probably not the only one that was pounding when finally a tall woman in a brown-striped (Barreges) dress with a shawl and a black velvet hat stepped out in front of the audience. She sat down without a greeting at a table with four candles, put her hat and scarf aside, ran her fingers through her hair, which curled down on both sides of her head, took out a small tablet and started her speech without any sign of fear; from time to time she looked at her notes. Her voice and presentation were very pleasant, and she knew how to give even the most frank expression a turn that could not offend even the most scrupulous.

She was often interrupted by applause, which was repeated at the end, and although many no doubt refused her teachings in their applause, I am convinced that everyone appreciated her personality and eloquence. Since, in the slave-states, it is enough to be known to be a liberal and philanthropist in order to have the whole world against you, it is easy to imagine that the entire city was put into an uproar by her lectures, and that all the lies that had been spread about her boiled up again, especially among her own sex, many of whom found the opportunity convenient to demonstrate their piety. Partly by this and some articles in the newspapers and partly as a consequence of there being only a few French-speaking persons present, who besides care very little about religion and understand very little English, her next two to three lectures in the French theatre were not as well attended, and I am convinced that in the slave-holding states she will have more difficulty in establishing an obvious following. Her previously mentioned attempt to gradually abolish slavery is supposed to have cost her 28,000 piaster.

I was unable to attend her last lecture due to an invitation I had received to visit a sugar plantation nine to ten miles out of town. Since they were still working at pressing, I did not want to miss this opportunity, since everything had ceased close to the city. Prior to the transfer of Louisiana to America, the production of sugar cane was completely unknown. The indigo plant, which, each year, was usually consumed by cabbage worms, and cotton were the only export articles of the almost unpopulated country. The many French immigrants from Santo Domingo first started planting sugar cane, and the great success with which their work was crowned brought in so many successors that the production of indigo and cotton completely ceased in the southern part of the state and only sugar cane was raised. The profit from this operation was so great already in 1828 that after the local consumption in the state was satisfied, more than 80,000 hogsheads of sugar and 40–50,000 barrels of syrup were exported, mainly to the northern United States. As long as this consumption exceeds the production by the southern states, there is an advantage to creating new plantations, since a high duty is paid on the import of foreign sugar. However, if it increases to a degree that foreign sale is necessary, it is hard to believe that the prices will fall below that which is reasonable, and new products must be considered.

The owner of the plantation to which I was invited with some friends, Mr. [John J.] Coiron, had sent us a beautiful and very light Vienna cart and fresh horses halfway, so that, since the road was good, we arrived after six hours, having passed many beautiful plantations and many ships in the river. A very small residence but a new and wonderful sugarhouse with a steam engine managed by a clever housekeeper reminded me of my father's sheep house. Mr. C. had owned the plantation for only two years, and he had named it *"Mon Secour,"* after having been almost ruined in the ownership of another one not far away, the soil of which was extremely poor. This is the worst part of starting a new development. One has to continually purchase land without knowing if the land is worth ten piaster or fifty cents. Everything is covered with forest standing half under water, making impossible any attempt of testing the soil beforehand. In the Antilles, where there is no frost to worry about, the sugar cane stands for eighteen months before it is pressed and is far more poisonous than here, where they have to harvest it every year. It remains on the root until it is taken to the press, and it cannot be cut ahead of time since the sun then would dry it out. It is the most juicy cane I have seen, not hollow, and with no marrow. It reaches a height of ten to twelve feet. The sugar press consists of three cylinders which are close together and driven by a wheel placed on the center one, so that two cylinders go in a direction opposite the third, and the sugar cane receives a double press by first passing between the two, and by rollers located behind they are passed back between the center ones and the third one.

The juice is thus pressed out, runs down into the pots and becomes thick by steaming out by boiling in five different stages. That is, the fire becomes gradually warmer under each kettle, and the sugar is then scooped from the fifth pot, where it is strengthened. After cooling, it is transferred to the hogsheads where crystallization takes place by placing the sediments of the syrup in cisterns placed below. In Mr. Coiron's sugar house, there were two batteries, or rows, of kettles, but only one worked day and night from the beginning of the process and to the end about two months later. During the previous harvest, he had made about 400 hogsheads of sugar. This year, however, he had cleared more land and put it into production, but he cannot expect that much since a damaging frost in Nov. had wrought unexpected damage to all the sugar plantations. Of these, some are getting only a half yield, and Louisiana as a whole can expect to get 80–90,000 fewer casks of sugar and syrup for export than last year. For St. Croix, which had a rich harvest, and which, with Louisiana supplies the northern states, this can only be a great advantage. Such a plantation with its eighty Negroes and apparatus can give an annual gross income of 24–30,000 piaster and is perhaps worth 130,000 piaster. At my departure the following day, I received a very friendly invitation to come back and spend two weeks with them. I doubt that it will happen, but it shows their hospitality, which is

A 19ᵗʰ Century Sugar Cane Plantation Mill

great all through the plantations. One must be careful not to talk in favor of freeing the slaves, since this is enough to become at odds with those who care the most. They have hundreds of reasons to defend their tainted cause, and, naturally, one is not better than the next. One feels pain in one's bones to see these unhappy beings night and day before a melting fire — without hope and prospect for a future. Two were chained together and dared not look up — they had followed their natural instinct and tried to get their freedom, and they are ashamed of looking their tormentors in the eye. That is how far a human being can be degraded.

In speaking of this sad case, I must touch on one connected to it. Lately, there have been many fires, and, because of the poor firefighting department in the city, a cotton press with 5,400 bales of cotton was lately consumed by fire, together with other buildings. The hand of the arsonist seemed obvious. Since they admit their flagrant injustice toward the Negroes and even against the freed mulattoes without ever wanting to admit it, it is always assumed, without good reason, that they are the arsonists. Consider that

47

all judges are white and that there is a completely different legal code for the colored, so that while a slave is punished by death just for raising his hand against a white, a white man is only fined 300 piaster for killing a slave. When one considers that the unfortunate souls must submit to all kinds of mistreatment and injustice without ever attaining any rights, one should, in truth, not wonder why the desire for revenge can awaken in the chest of even the most wretched, and that it is expressed in any possible manner. One can only wonder why it does not take place more often, and that desperation does not cause more violent acts. My God! What would I do under such conditions! I shall abstain from any kind of argument about this most sad subject; it makes me become half-Negro.

With all of this, it cannot be denied that many slave-owners treat their Negroes well, and that the slave has no cares his entire life, but in order for this to become an honor for the master and true reassurance for the slave, one probably must...[*sic*] about self-interest or love of mankind drives the former, and whether the latter thinks no deeper than another drudge. By such a scrutiny would, to the disgrace of humanity, hardly be found more than one philanthropic master or thinking slave out of 100. What is worst and most embarrassing is that, in the southern United States, there is no indication that improvements will ever take place. The fear of a Negro rebellion closes any admittance of colored free men, who, in a free state, lack civil rights and thus, must be enemies of their oppressors.

In the state of Georgia, they have gone so far that lately they have enacted a law stipulating a heavy penalty for anyone teaching coloreds to read and write! This is to prevent printed or written human rights principles from causing a rebellion. And here in Louisiana, a prohibition has lately been issued against freeing Negroes unless they are moved out of the country. Thus, the government forces the colored people themselves to use any opportunity they have to rebel as the only means to gain civil liberties. On Christmas Eve, there was fear of an uprising and all the citizens were alerted. And, as is the case at each fire, they are afraid that it could be an organized plot by the Negroes to take advantage of such an occasion for their rebellion. Almost every day there is an auction of Negroes at the market. I decided to attend one and am almost regretting my curiosity, since nothing can be more upsetting and degrading to humanity. I did, however, stay till the end and thus, became a witness to how they treat these unfortunate creatures as animals. One Negro family consisting of husband, wife and two children were sold and put aside. Someone else who wished to buy them went and examined them the way one would examine horses and cows, and then made a bid of twenty-five piaster higher. The seller accepted the offer and said to the unfortunate ones, while pointing to the new buyer: "*viola votre maitre*" [indicating the enslaved family's new master]. The new owner brought them to the others he had bought who were awaiting his further orders.

That is the way they trade in people in a free country! This despicable slavery is also the biggest stumbling block between the northern and southern states, and, if a breach should ever happen between them, this will probably become one of the most difficult things to set right, since the north hates slavery. In the south, it will be impossible to settle it quietly, and the defense of it is too well organized to change without having a total revolution. It will cost streams of blood as it did in Santo Domingo. If the slave owners would gradually give in, much could possibly be salvaged, but right now, they want to wait their time out, and the result will be that they will lose everything. Although I have been more long-winded regarding this subject than I intended to be, there are, unfortunately, tomes that could be written about it, and I am afraid to think that there might be occasion to return to it in the course of this diary. It is a sad stain on a country about which one could truly say that personified wisdom has had the driver's seat in the legislature, and where political freedom rules to the greatest extent of the word.

The condition of the Indians, the former absolute masters of the country, is also a cloud on the bright sky of North America, which, in itself, in the eyes of many, darkens its twenty-five stars. By wars, treaties and sales, they have been continually driven farther and farther from the coasts; as the numbers of immigrants increased and their cultivation of the land spread, the various tribes shrunk back to living in some forests and mountains in the various states, the occupation of which, although guaranteed by treaties with the United States government, can, at any time, be disputed by land-greedy neighbors, who from all sides by violence and deceit drive them farther and farther into the mountains. Several of these tribes are not decreasing in number, no matter how they have been objects of warfare and their neighbors' strongest weapon, liquor. Everywhere they refuse to mingle with the white population or subject themselves to the laws of the state in which they live. This has led the president, in his latest speech, at the opening of Congress, to recommend that they research whether it would be advisable in order to prevent mistreatment of the Indians and to promote advancement in agriculture in the areas where they live in the various states, to send all of them (almost 600,000–800,000) to the unpopulated forests and areas west of the Mississippi and, there, guarantee them perpetual incorruptible rights to a certain wide territory. Without waiting for the result of this, the state of Georgia has already written a law which, against the treaties of the United States, forces the Indians, within a certain period of time, to subject themselves to the laws of the state or leave the state.

This very unfair decision activated all philanthropists of the north, and especially female ones, so that lately there have been showers of petitions on Congress asking the government of the United States to protect the natives against this unfair line of action by the state of Georgia. The result of this is still unknown.

Here in New Orleans, the Indians, who come to peddle the results of their hunting and labors, are a sad sight. Wrapped in dirty blankets, they sit around a fire in the least cool air and drink liquor as long as they have any or enough money to buy any. Later on, you see them, both men and women, lying completely naked in the streets, so drunk that they are unable to move. Liquor is the most potent weapon one can use against the unfortunate natives, and a truly humane government would, at least, have a ban on selling intoxicating drinks to them, no matter how difficult it would be to enforce. This, however, does not take place and thus, the Indian population will probably, noticeably decrease unless they do not associate with the whites, which is difficult for them not to do. Numerous missionaries who have been sent to be among them have so far, in vain, attempted to bring these hordes to some kind of civilization, although in some places they are not disorganized and are tilling their soil by the use of plows. Attempts have been made several times to give the wild children an education, separated from their tribe, but they either die from homesickness for their forests, or they run away when it is thought that they no longer think about their former homes. Some of the older ones have been taken into homes as servants. They have stayed there for extended times and been well behaved, but there are several examples where, by the smallest event, where they fairly or unfairly felt they had been offended, they, during the night, had killed all inhabitants of the house and fled into the woods.

Since any kind of mixing is thus impossible, it is natural that the colonists envy them [for] their ownership of large stretches of land, and that they attempt to make it fertile by through all means driving the Indians away from it, and it is undeniable that, if they could be sure that they would not be disturbed on the other side of the Mississippi, they would be just as happy there. But the population of the United States is increasing with giant steps, and it is impossible to deny the possibility that in the future there will be new states formed in the immense stretches of land from the Mississippi to the ocean with fertile soil for agriculture. In that case, could the Indians expect to enjoy freedom and protection? I consider that it is likely that the former masters of the land, numbering two to three million, which has already dwindled to one-third, in time, will completely disappear from the globe.

The entire standing army of the United States consists of no more than 6,000 men during peacetime! There can hardly be a stronger test of the wisdom by which the constitution of the land was drawn. Since the president, as the executive power, is commander-in-chief of the army, a large army in the hands of an imperious president could be dangerous, not only for the finances of the country, but also for its freedom. Each state has its own citizens trained to defend their country in an emergency, but in no case are they to leave it to wage war outside its borders. Of all the state militias, none has done the country a bigger service than Louisiana's, although none was a combination of descendants of people from several nations. It was during England's unjust war against the United States during the years 1812 to 1815 that the citizens of Louisiana saved not only their own state, but probably also many others in the union, if not all of them. In December 1814, England landed 12–14,000 men a few miles south of New Orleans. They intentionally chose a location where the land-owning population and slavery gave them the biggest chance of luck. They, therefore, immediately sent proclamations to the city, but only in French and Spanish, in which they talked about the disease of American suppression, and with promises of everything good if the citizens would support them.

Unfortunately for them, English politics were too well-known in Louisiana, which besides was happy under its current constitution, for the proclamation to have any effect other than a firm determination to strongly resist the enemy of the state, but nothing had been prepared to do this. The United States had absolutely no troops in Louisiana, and New Orleans was without the simplest fortifications and had only its citizens, who were not at all disciplined and even less armed for its defense. They had at most 2,000 men against 14,000 of England's best troops, ones who had fought in the war against Spain and were led by Wellington's brother-in-law, Sir Edward Peckenham. However, communications were sent to all sides about the English invasion, with pleas to all neighboring states for assistance. Help did not fail to come and, before the English had unloaded all of their war materiel and personnel, etc., the current president, General Jackson, had already arrived with the militias from several states, but very few regular army troops. He made all possible preparations for defense, and, when the English advanced toward the city on December 23, he met them halfway and forced them to retreat. The entire English force had not yet arrived, and, since from false reports they thought that the defense of the city far exceeded their strength, they did not want to risk a new attack before they had all of their forces together. If this had not happened and the English had gone against the city immediately after landing, there is no doubt that they would have taken it without lifting a sword, since against a disciplined army, individual courage is of little help when leadership, training and numbers are considered.

Fate, which so wonderfully watched over the country, wanted it differently. The English did not attempt a new attack until January 8, 1815, but that was with determination and with the full strength of their 12–14,000 men. But the Americans had not been idle in the meantime, with Jackson's strong spirit inspiring everyone, help rushed in from all sides every day. Entrenchments went up between the river and the cypress forests, the only route the English could take to the city, a line of almost a half mile behind which fortification he wanted to resist their attack. The Americans had only a few cannons, and nobody who knew how to operate them. But necessity is the mother of invention: there were some pirates in the city prison awaiting execution; Jackson freed them and placed them at the cannons, and their service was very effective. On January 8, as mentioned, the English attacked after the Americans had just finished their fortifications the evening before. Their full strength was less than 6,000 men with all kinds of weapons, but most of them were excellent marksmen, and Jackson trusted them, and the outcome proved that it was not without reason. It had rained during the night and the soil, mostly clay, was wet and slippery. This made the attack on the American fortification difficult for the English even if it had been less well defended. Already in the first attack, more than half of the attacking column fell before the accurate firing of the Americans. Among them were many high-ranking officers, including the leader, General Peckenham. He died a few seconds later in the shade of four big oak trees, which for later generations will bear witness to his and his country's shameful politics and derisive defeat. New attacks followed, but they were all repelled, with enormous losses for the English, who were finally forced, after one of their generals had been killed and the other one wounded, completely to give up the attempt, the result of which crowned the American weapons with immortal honor and deeply wounded the English intolerable arrogance.

The total loss to the Americans on this honorable day was only ninety-seven dead and wounded, while the English admit that it cost them more than 2,700 men.

The observance of this day, which I attended, and it made a deep impression on me, and gave me the opportunity to give this short description of its origin. I never felt less tempted to consider myself superior to these common soldiers than by watching "*La legion de la Louisiana*" pass in revue before the state governor, who, in plain black clothing and his hat in hand, was surrounded by his staff officers, while the troops presented arms and the music played famous French revolutionary marches, which instilled a special joy in me. It proved to me true greatness in contrast to European glitter and tinsel.

This American principle, which observes only the essentials and scorns nonsensical matters of secondary importance, was evident all over. Thus, all of the old states have maintained many of the names of towns, counties and parishes that were given to them during the English supremacy, to wit, almost all estates in north America, and even institutions, are still called by Royal names. Here in New Orleans, all the old streets are named after the royal French family, and, since the Americans took possession of the country and the city, the only change made was to place on each corner the name "Street" instead of "Rue." Now they are called "Bourbon St.," "Chartres St.," "Conde St.," "Orleans St.," etc. Even "Rue de l' Amour" and "Rue des Français" are on some corners called "Amour St." and "Français St.," but they have never wanted to rename them completely. Maybe nobody even thought about that. It was different in the French revolution. There they thought more about nonsensical matters than the proper ones, and the difference between the serious English and the lighter French character is never seen more clearly. Thus, America is the most fortunate republic and France was the most wretched one.

At the end of last month, the subscription balls began here. Since there, as previously mentioned, are very few parties here and thus, no balls in private homes, and one can only, in a few places, see anyone who favors pleasures more than here, it is natural that it has been necessary to think of other means "*a voir and etre vu*" [to see and to be seen].

In 1826, the owner of the French theater built a very nice ballroom next door. It had a number of rooms for public use, and soon a party was formed by fathers who had daughters to give away to young gentlemen who wished to make their acquaintances. They decided to hold eight balls during the winter at a cost of 50 piaster per person, an enormous price, which assured a select group. It was a success, but when they found that for every four ladies there was only one dancing man, they finally decided that the pleasure should not be concentrated around good eating and drinking, which the older ones preferred, but on dancing, which required youth, not only of the fair sex. The evening meal was canceled in order to make admittance easier. The price was gradually reduced until it is now fifteen piaster. Many young people are now subscribers, and these balls are now made up of everything the city and surrounding area possess of fashion.

Although surrounded by this elegant company, a poor dancer such as I would still get bored if the inner value of the party were its only virtue. But when one can imagine that on my not so few excursions in the world, I have never seen such a gathering of beautiful women, which makes up the majority of those present, it is not so strange that I, as any other stranger would, found it pleasant and enjoyable. The ladies were as luxuriously dressed and with no less taste than in France; in general, they dance well, but they lack very much the ease in conversation which does not silence a stranger who may be unfamiliar with family relations in town and its "*Cancans*," and who does not feel like talking a la Ditmar about the weather. This is torture to a dancer when he, so to speak, must pull a 'yes' or 'no' out of the mouth of the most beautiful creature. This happens often here and, when one sometimes meets a lady who answers in more than a monosyllable, a Creole accent often creeps in and this robs one of an illusion which was very promising. The mixture of French- and English-speaking, especially among the fair sex, is also here a big difficulty, since these balls, so to speak, are the only ones to be found all winter in the better classes. Although the American population is just as large as the French, there were seldom more than six to eight English-speaking ladies, who kept themselves completely separated from the others and only danced with their own. The absence of the American beauties was, however, no loss to the ball, since very few of them could claim this name, especially next to the French New Orleans.

Besides these subscription balls, which are made up of the best quality in the vicinity, there are many others to which any white and fairly well-dressed man can participate in for his piaster, but where everyone of the fair sex is colored, although the majority of them are as white as their female neighbors, who show much contempt, and many are just as beautiful, if not more so. It is no wonder that the young men in town seldom stay away from here, where most acquaintances are made; that leaves many young women unmarried and many a wife deserted. All of these girls prefer to live with a white man over marriage to one of their own, with whom they want as little to do as the white women with them.

Although there are many virtuosos of talent on many instruments, concerts are rare and, with their high cost, impossible, if they are not followed by a ball, and then they are only successful for the Labat family (our naval expert fellow-traveler, whom I have mentioned above), since all of the beauties in town are their pupils, and the art is just in enticing them. The men will show up. This year there was no public concert, however, much to my regret, since I had an opportunity to ascertain the talent of the youngest as a singer and the eldest as a piano player. Mr. Labat was courteous enough to invite me to a musical morning entertainment, although he knew how little I knew about the art, together with two young sons of Count Otranto (the famous Fouche), who are traveling through America and have stayed here for about a month, and a few other foreigners. Since Mrs. Labat runs a musical instrument store, everything was performed on the very best instruments, and especially, a duet on two pianofortes from the best factory in Paris, and after a new invention, was excellent.

Of strange foreigners here at present, besides the above-mentioned, there is the former Secretary of State of the United States, Mr. Henry Clay, a very talented man, who could perhaps become the next president of the union. He is very popular, especially since he is anti-Jackson, and several of the new administration's measures are very unpopular, especially the promotion to public positions of all of Jackson's creatures at the expense of several thousand heads of families and honest men who were terminated without notice. A great fuss was made of Henry Clay and everybody wanted to wait on him. I did not know anything about the man and his principles beyond that which his friends and advocates told me, and which, in a republic, is a very suspicious authority. It appears to me to be an obvious falsehood, which absolutely goes against my principles, to go up and greet a man who maybe does not have anything in common with me. I, therefore, refused repeated offers to be introduced to him. It finally came to a point where I hated to refuse, and I went up with some others. After the visit, I am still unable to judge the man, since he only had a moment for us and then turned to someone else with whose relatives he was acquainted. He was a tall, skinny man with a face which, in my opinion, did not have much expression. If he ever becomes the president, the acquaintance will be of interest — to me.

This month the weather has been as a beautiful as May at home, and often so warm that one prefers to go out in the afternoon when the sun has cooled off a little. I enjoyed on my frequent walks here in January seeing children in the streets in shirt sleeves and bare legs. There were also roses in bloom, and the orange trees were full of ripe fruit.

Henry Clay
(1777 – 1852)

Since my arrival, I have been busy finishing the business that was the main purpose of my trip, in order to try to avoid having to go to Mexico. But hardly had one difficulty been resolved before another popped up, and I found it necessary, against the advice of all of my friends here, who wanted me to start a lawsuit here — a decision which no doubt would have been pleasant for me, but unknown if it would have been the opposite for my friends in Le Havre — namely, to take the first ship for Tampico. This was at the end of February, an opportunity was open in a few days, which became several weeks, and I did not leave New Orleans until March 14, in one of the most wonderful American schooners, with a cabin arranged as on a packet-boat.

Onward to Mexico

After a crossing of eight days, we got in sight of the Mexican coast, and, on Saturday, we took a pilot aboard and came in across the terrible sand bars into the river. After having gotten used to seeing the Indians in New Orleans, and without knowing that there was a difference between the North American and Mexican natives, it made a strange but, at the same time, pleasant impression on me that the first useful Mexicans I saw were Indians, namely almost twenty of them in the pilot's launch. He was also an Indian, and they were all big and good-looking fellows, some without shirts and only in underpants, while others wore both and everything was very clean. Since the Indians in the United States are still in their original wild condition and are of no use to society, I could have no better surprise than to see them being useful in a country, the civilization of which I had very little knowledge, and where they made up the majority of the population.

On both sides of the river's mouth, which was 500 to 600 feet wide, there were remains of poor fortifications built of earth and poles where bloody battles had taken place at the last visit of the Spaniards. In order to prevent the enormous smuggling activities which had taken place during the early years of the republic, a mass of formalities and searches take place, which are no worse than in France and England. There is almost one mile from the town to the mouth of the river, but none of the passengers were allowed to leave the ship, which was not permitted to go in until the following evening. The river is very beautiful, with forests on both sides, and on one side are some hills.

The Mexican general Santa Anna had a battery erected there to protect the entire city, which was under Spanish control. The Spaniards did not notice anything until it was completed, and they came under fire from it. It looks good at the top of the hill, which is completely covered with trees. The city is beautifully located, but does not look good from the river. It has only been here for five years, or rather, five years ago, many of the inhabitants moved from a small town a few miles away to this location, which was thought to be healthier and a better location for trading. Considering the short time the city has been

Antonio de Santa Anna
(1794 – 1876)

in existence, one could wonder about its significance in a country where foreigners of low standing find very little encouragement to immigrate. Even if it is not more important, it is reasonable to think that it will grow, especially if yellow fever does not come every year. Last year, it was hard on the Spaniards, whose bad luck could have been the fever rather than the sword of the Mexicans. Since the battles in the city damaged many of the buildings, almost all of them had been restored, and the streets in the center of town did not look too bad. Almost all of the houses are one story with a flat roof. Most of them have only doors, and, where there are windows, there is no glass in them, but only iron bars, since the heat requires that they have a breeze from all sides. The streets are straight, and some are starting to look pretty nice, since the foreign merchants who make up the majority are having their own buildings constructed.

Tampico is important as an import center for foreign goods, since it supplies all of northern Mexico, and, since the English are the primary manufacturers, it is natural that most of the main merchants are English. The Germans also play an important role, however, and there are three important German warehouses all manned by young people speaking the same language. Most of them are from Bremen and Hamburg, young knights of fortune, who came during the best time of the year and, for the most part, ignore the bad. They live the European way, and I fear that, during the summer, many of them will suffer due to their carelessness. In the meantime, the yellow fever is far from what it is in New Orleans, maybe for the simple reason that there are fewer victims here. As mentioned earlier, those who are born here, or who have had the fever, are not subject to the sickness and it's sad consequences.

To return to the city — for each of the fifty or perhaps 100 estates built of stone or half-timbered, there is a three-fold number of the most miserable shacks that serve as shelter for the lower class, who live on daily wages. These shacks are most often built of bamboo, which is placed no closer together than one can see through them, that is, without windows, and a door of bamboo or miserable boards tied together, as are all parts of the shacks, without a single nail. The roof is made of reeds so long that it moves with the slightest breeze. Other huts consist of only three posts placed in the ground with the ends together. Two sides are thatched with reeds from top to bottom and the third side is open, but the furnishings are no temptation to anybody. The bed is a wide bench with a hide on. The dirt with a few rocks for a fireplace is sofa, chair and table. Domestic utensils consist of a stone pot or maybe two, a pan for baking tortillas (small pancakes from cornmeal), and a hollow stone for grinding the corn. It is difficult to imagine the frugality of a Mexican: they live almost entirely on tortillas and a few sweet beans called *frijoles*, and Spanish pepper, hot as can be, their only spice. Here, we are talking about the lowest class of people, those better off have, no doubt, more varied food, but one must go up quite a bit on the social ladder before one finds bread instead of tortillas on the table.

Bread is completely unknown outside the big cities, and knives and forks are luxury articles, even in the so-called better houses, one uses the most natural [implements]. This is so literal that at the evening meal of a ball I attended in Tampico, hosted by a German merchant, none of the Mexican ladies ate anything, but took home what they could. The reason was that there were no tortillas and, not knowing how to handle knives and forks, they were ashamed to use their fingers in the presence of strangers. These Mexican ladies were enchanting, especially striking when one comes from New Orleans, and I had difficulty keeping from laughing out loud. Their hair, which in New Orleans they knew how to set with great taste, was absolutely flat with a thin braid and a few small curls, and their dresses were in all different colors, most without a tied waist and shape[d] like water bags. A few had nice feet, but ugly shoes, which ruined everything. All in all there were no more than ten to twelve dancing ladies who, instead of refreshments between dances, as with us, were offered a lighted cigar by their partners by which they lit theirs made from paper, and smoked with great delight. Their simplicity went so far that the man they had danced with would lead them outside when "nature called," staying and conversing with them while they took care of it.

This sounds a little strange to European ears, but maybe not to Spanish ears. Yet it is possible that in their natural simplicity they are just as chaste and good as our women. Custom and upbringing is everything and any judgment depends on the circumstances of the eyes of the judge. No matter how much this crude behavior offended me, I am unable to say that a person who is free of all prejudice would give our fine and exaggerated manners the advantage over these unrefined and natural ladies. I left the party already before midnight, since I felt the need to be extra careful in this climate, and I also had the trump that I was feeling perfect the next day, while almost all of the Germans, who had been drinking till the break of dawn, were so miserable that they could hardly see. I fear that when the hot and unhealthy season arrives some of them will never see their homeland again.

There is a small garrison in Tampico. The size is hard to determine since they never march or have maneuvers. I have never seen a more miserable army. White, brown, yellow and black faces mixed together, with poor canvas equipment that is so dirty it is almost black. Most are barefoot with sandals, which is the common footwear for the lower class. Man to man, the Mexicans could never win over the Spanish, who made the last attack. These were excellent troops, who only retreated from a terribly superior force and the even more terrible sickness. It is still strange that, although Mexicans consider the Spanish to be the only nation outside of Mexico that deserves respect, and, in any regards, is better than all the rest, they still love their independence, or rather unrestrained conditions, enough that the Spanish general [Isidro] Barradas, who, in his proclamation, promised a half doubloon [eight specie dollars] to any Mexican who came to his side, he was unable to get even one to desert. From this, he soon realized what course his mad expedition would take, since it was primarily based on the hope that all of the dissatisfied people in the republic would come streaming to the Spanish flag as soon as it was planted on the coast of Mexico. With all of this, there is hardly any doubt that a well-organized Spanish force of 15–20,000 men could advance straight to the capital. But such an endeavor must be well managed and not depend on an *arradas* [perhaps referring to *entradas (historical)* an armed incursion of Spanish conquistadors into American territories].

Another question is whether the Spanish would be able to hang on to any part of the country if they once conquered it, and this any impartial person would consider to be impossible. Just as in Denmark, everyone here would be dependent on the state for a living. One thousand people would have high pensions because they carried arms against the Spanish during the revolution. They benefit from having a weak government. Another thousand, mainly officers, might be on active duty but do nothing. Their number is so high that several regiments have more officers than ordinary soldiers, and they are also in favor of a central government that will not dare reduce their numbers or cut their salaries for fear of a revolution. This would no doubt happen with just the slightest change. In short, the patriotism of most of the Mexicans [that is, the higher classes, or the ones descending from the Spanish] is, to the highest degree, only self-interest. This has been the case on hundreds of occasions in the many movements that have already stirred the country since its first political existence. I believe that, at the present time, the country is as well governed as it can possibly be under its present constitution, since the most capable men in the republic are heading the government. But due to lack of character and strength, they will probably be lost as has happened to so many of their predecessors. They are afraid to punish political criminals, since a revolution, which could always happen, could bring them under the governance of the party they are now suppressing, and which would not hesitate to get even.

The constitution of Mexico is modeled after the United States, but they have lost sight of the enormous difference in the political education of the people of the two countries. While the United States from the beginning of its independence has enjoyed all of the blessings flowing from a free government, formed according to the needs of the people, the United Mexican States have never been discomfited, not as a result of anything missing in the constitution, but by its application toward such a people. As difficult as it would be for the United States to exist under the rule of a monarch, it would be difficult for Mexico to be at ease under a republican constitution in which each state is sovereign, and time will teach them that all of the new republican republics will continue to tear out their innards until they find their Bonaparte, who, under the mask of freedom, maybe could swing the scepter of autocracy and force them to be happy.

Let us return to Tampico: my business there is taking a most favorable turn, but not until I agreed to make a trip to Mexico City to assist in recovering the means for which I had made a Tampico house reliable and on which there had been a 60 percent loss.

Such a trip, although only seventy to eighty miles, in a land where no kinds of public conveniences can be found, and where, with the exception of a few stretches, there are no roads but only foot paths across mountains and rivers, is no small endeavor. Even for the natives and those familiar with it, considerable preparations are required, so it is even more difficult for a stranger. The first thing needed for this trip are the animals, and, as difficult as it is to sell them after the trip is completed, which I later experienced, it is just as difficult to find what one wants when the trip begins. Then, there are the servants; most travelers who have been murdered or robbed underway could thank their attendants for it. Since I had no desire to find a reason for such gratefulness, I had to pay a Portuguese, who spoke very good English and Spanish and was an honest man, 1½ piaster per day in addition to his board, horse and accessories. Besides him, I found a Mexican, who had two old horses, good animals from whom I could expect no evil. For my own use, I bought a horse and a mule, plus the needed equipment for 139 piaster, a horse for my Portuguese for twenty-six, and I borrowed a mule. Under these circumstances, I started my trip to Mexico with my two servants on April 4. They had told me much about robbers, and the most terrible scars on the limbs of some acquaintances were witnesses to the reality that they existed. It was, therefore, necessary to go armed; besides two pistols, which I had brought along from New Orleans, I bought a double-barrel rifle and borrowed a saber. Armed as well with a couple of empty pistol holders tied to my saddle, I was going to defy all of Mexico's robbers and rogues.

Tampico is located on the northern bank of the river, so that everyone traveling south is forced to cross the river. I had to send my two- and four-legged animals across a day in advance, since bridges and ferries are contraband in this blessed country, and all beasts of burden have to swim across. Many get lost, since the distance is great and the current is often so strong that the animals get tired midways. Fortunately, mine got across without being lost, and I crossed on a sailboat the following morning to the old town, or so-called Pueblo Viejo, a distance of about three miles, into a small river with beautiful banks with the most curious and strange plants clear down to the water, which serves as an outflow from a small lake by which the town is located. The water in it is so shallow that only with difficulty did we get across it in our little dinghy, and, during the summer, it is completely dry in many places. This causes emanations which contribute to making the place unwholesome. There was not a blacksmith in all of Tampico who could shoe my animals, but I was told that there were several in Pueblo Viejo, and that I should have my people take care of it before I arrived. I was thus very annoyed when I heard that there was not a blacksmith, and that it would be a long distance to the next one. I expected that my animals would go lame since the road was very rocky. This was the beginning of much unpleasantness awaiting me on this trip, for which even a rather truthful description by several acquaintances in Tampico could have prepared me.

The first day of my trip was short. Already, by five o'clock, we got to some small houses, where we decided to spend the night and then really get going the next morning. We could not hope to reach an inn until about two days of travel from Mexico. We settled for the night under a projecting roof from the best house where I had asked about some supper and some corn for the horses. I was happy not to hear for the first time the oft repeated "*no hai*" [we don't have any]. Luckily enough, I had brought a small box of sea biscuits, a ham, cheese and some bottles of gin for my people, as well as a couple of pounds of chocolate, which is easily prepared on the trip. Besides this, my appetite is not that great, and I did not fear the eternal "*no hai*" as did my companions. They then searched the neighborhood and finally located a miserable shack where we could enjoy a good meal consisting of *frijoles* [red beans], tortillas, and even meat. I went down and took a look at the apartment and shall hurry up and give a short description of it and its inhabitants. As soon as I got closer, I was met by a band of at least a dozen starved dogs of all breeds and dimensions who would not let me come close until waiting for five minutes for me to express my "*Buenos tardes, señoritas!*" ["Good evening, my ladies"] to two pretty creatures who filled the opening to the shack — a door would be considered an extravagance.

The residence of these beauties was made of materials which would have been an honor for our first ancestors, and, in seeing it, one would not need much poetic blood to retreat to that innocent age, especially in regard to the clothing and domestic utensils of the occupants. The shack consisted of sticks leaning against each other and covered with leaves, and the furnishings were a bench or two made from the roughest materials and covered with a dried cow hide, and these also served as beds. A small, low piece of wood, which was offered to me as a chair, and a stump, which served as a table, were outside the hut. Three boulders the size of a head made up the fireplace, which was covered by a clay pan for baking the wonderful tortillas, while a clay pot on one side of the fire contained the beans. A stick on the other side served as spit for the sun-dried strips of meat which were to form the main part of our treats. Behind the fire squatted the eldest of the ladies, dressed in a shift and skirt. She held a stick in each hand, one to keep the starved dogs away from the meat, and the other to stir in the pot and to turn the tortillas. Next to her, at the other edge of the opening to the hut, her daughter kneeled, grinding corn for the divine tortillas. That is a hard job, which they are so used to doing that they most certainly would not consider using the most simple and easy machine one could give them, although it would make it so much better. The beauty I mentioned who sat and worked behind the stone was about 22 to 25 years old, but already had many children, who played outside the hut after getting tired of gawking at me. Their mother felt the strain of her work and, in order to make it easier, she had shed her innermost piece of clothing, which she had tied around her loins, and thus, left the entire upper part to free observation by the naturalist. She was a brown Indian, shapely with pendent breasts. My presence did not bother her in the least, and I made sure that my glance did not cause her to blush.

In most of the villages, there are absolutely no inns, and, where there is one to be found, you cannot expect to find such a superfluous piece of furniture as a bed. All you can find at one of the better places is a table and a straw mat on which a tired traveler can rest, and often he is so tired that he forgets that he has ever been more comfortable. I was not quite of this opinion when I made this trip, so I had a collapsible bed frame with canvas, which I could unfold when I got lodging, and I felt wonderful doing that. Besides having a softer bed than the earth or a table, I also avoided the mass of creeping and flying insects that can be considered the biggest torment to a traveler in this blessed country. This is only at the coast, however; inland, the most wonderful and healthy climate, is combined with a complete relief from damaging insects. The coast has many; besides scorpions and millipedes, whose stings are deadly, there are spiders called tarantulas, completely black and hairy. They sting at the slightest touch and inject a poison that is deadlier than that of the scorpion. Along the coast are also the bloodthirsty mosquitoes, very much like ours in size and gray color, and they are so voracious that it is impossible to shut your eyes all night if you do not have a net around you. Fortunately, I had one, and it also served as a shield against many curious eyes, which could never get enough gaping at such a foreign animal as I must have seemed to them.

In addition to the mosquitoes, after traveling for several days inland there is a kind of aphid called *grappa*, which will land on you by the thousands when you go through bushes. They will find their way through the seams and any openings in one's clothes and into one's skin, where they bury their heads and suck as long as one lets them alone. These small animals, about the size of a bedbug, will swell up till they are the size of the outer joint of an index finger before they drop off. They are now completely blue and the head and the six legs are hardly visible against the large body. Those thick brutes can be seen hanging on the stomachs and legs of all kinds of animals, who suffer much from them, and they were absolutely the biggest plague on this trip. One of my acquaintances in Tampico, who had recently returned from Mexico City, had inflammation in his legs from their bites. There is a danger in trying to rip them off that the head will stay under the skin and immediately start swelling up. After all that, I had heard I was very careful and brought my gin along to wash my skin, which would cause them to fall off. However, I relied mainly on my own blood, which so far had seemed to be tasty to similar predators, and on my white riding britches, which enabled me to see the enemy, and thus gave me an opportunity to get him off before he had time to dig in. It was not a bad calculation; my servants could hardly stand it for itching and pain, but I only suffered one night from these insects. The first thing a Mexican does when he comes to a resting place is to roll up his pants legs and pick his legs — this comes before eating and drinking for both animal and man.

Our next day-trip was through palm and coco woods and ended in a village on top of a mountain overgrown with the most beautiful scrubs, teeming with thousand-colored flowers. The coco-trees are small in this area, and, instead of a big nut in a thick shell which contains the fruit, there are many small ones whose kernels have the same taste. The palm forests, which were exciting to me at first, soon became terribly monotonous. The trees are tall, but without branches and only fans on top. The tree itself is so soft that it is of very little use. On the entire stretch, we saw fewer than ten houses and met just a few Indians here and there who gave us information about the road, since the route was strange not only to me but also to my servants. There are three roads to Mexico City from Tampico. One goes across the mountains and is only used during the rainy season when the others are impassable. Another one, which is called the best one, is the longest, that is why I chose it, I was now...[sic] me ahead on, and besides had assured me was the best one, but above all, a road where I would be able to find corn for my animals, water above all else, and also something for us to eat. It is far from common to be able to find water for one's livestock during the dry season, and one must often, especially in the western part of the country, ride miles to find it and then pay ½ real [almost twelve rds] per animal being watered. Regarding corn, which was supposed to be easy to buy everywhere, it was just the opposite. Some places they would let me have it for an equal weight in piaster. In the villages, you were lucky to find any, even at unreasonable prices, but in some houses, I got the sad reply: "*no hai,*" and soon got used to that as far as our own needs went.

The last Spanish attack and the presence of the Mexican army, which was advancing against it, were blamed for the high prices and the shortage of even the most basic food items. I think that more chickens than Spaniards have been sacrificed on this occasion. The main reason could probably be found in the carelessness and laziness of the inhabitants. The larger haciendas or tenant farms find it more profitable to raise cattle, which they let loose in the forests and meadows, rather than till the fields. Thus, it was only in a few places on the enormous stretches I passed through that I saw any tilled fields. In order to get the grass to grow better and greener in the forests, it is customary to burn the old when it gets close to the rainy season. I am already passing through many areas where the earth and all bushes and trees are black and scorched as far as the eye can see. This was far from pleasant, and I was happy by the end of my third day's travel to reach a bamboo and other kinds of forest where this did not take place. It is now getting hillier, and tall mountains can be seen in the far distance. From time to time, this creates the most beautiful views, and the rich vegetation is witness to what this country could become if it fell into better hands. An important hindrance to the development and wealth of the country must not be ignored, and that is the difficulty in acquiring the means to transport the produce of the soil. Strangely enough, Mother Nature has appeared to give unfair treatment to this otherwise favored country. It almost completely lacks navigable rivers or the means of substituting with canals or roads at a reasonable cost. For that reason, the only means of transportation have been mules and donkeys, which makes it difficult, if not downright impossible, to reap the wealth by circulating the natural or artistic creations.

Although this is only the beginning of April, almost all fruit trees, which grow wild along the road, have finished blossoming, and the lemon and orange trees, which are plentiful all over, had fruit, as did the walnuts. Thus, there is no shortage of the most beautiful flowers I have ever seen. I came through entire forests, the tops of which were covered with the most beautiful pink flowers one can imagine. And all the shrubbery had a mass of the prettiest bells and flowers; the countless and incomprehensibly beautiful colors could only be compared with the colors of the countless birds that unceasingly soared above my head and filled the air with song and screech. The parrots joined in the melody, and the ears had to suffer from what the eyes enjoyed of the looks of the pretty green, red and yellow colors which adorned these birds. A great number of small hummingbirds flew among the flowers.

On Maundy Thursday, the 8th, I arrived in Ticontepic, a small town located on a high mountain, which was difficult to reach, by a steep road full of sharp stones. The mountain itself is overgrown with forests and shrubbery, and in the lower regions, with the most majestic trees of various sorts, completely unknown in northern Europe. As we got closer to town, we met many men and women young and old, all in their Sunday clothes and very clean. They came from the church, and the town itself was crowded with farmers all dressed up. Among them some ran about in fantastic costumes. I soon learned that on the following day, Good Friday, they were to play the roles of Pharisees and Jews in a procession where the plot represents the happenings in Gethsemane with Judas' treason. Today, Maundy Thursday, the institution of Holy Communion and the washing of feet took place in the church. I decided to stay there for the day to witness this ceremony as well as to get my horses shod by two young men in their church clothes, who said that they understood that it was sacrilegious on the holiday to do such work, but out of kindness and for a few piaster they would do it.

The church, a large building that looked exactly like a barn, was crowded with people who sang, or rather shouted, one louder than the other. It was decorated with many green branches and ribbons in various colors, and, to one side, was a terrible picture of Christ, made of wood and with blood painted in all directions and mutilated to a degree that made people shiver by the sight of it. This was carried in the procession and guarded by two men dressed, I presume, in their idea of Romans with long lances. Time and again, one of them beat a drum and the other one blew a horn as hard as he could. This was a unique way to perform a service. Meanwhile, the priest went around and washed the feet of twelve old people, who sat in a circle, and then he served them an unbelievable portion of tortillas and other nice dishes, while the gaping multitude shouted and crossed itself from time to time. I did not see the slightest indication of edification or solemnity in this entire ceremony, which probably lasted for two hours, after which a procession was formed with the mayor and council following, walking all through the town. I regret that I was unable to watch this in Mexico City, where it would probably have had a more reverent atmosphere.

The following day was to me truly a "Long Friday" (the Danish name for Good Friday), and my companions did not neglect to assure me that it was because we were traveling on such a holiday. I was not far from regretting it myself, although for a different reason. I had been assured that by traveling one day further we would be able to reach a town named Asonte, located at the base of high mountains that we were to cross. My route map, which I had brought along from Tampico, mentioned another location on this side, and we actually reached the latter about three o'clock. About a half hour before my Mexican informed me that his horse had gone lame, and by the time we reached the place, the poor animal was unable to move a foot and we could see that it was suffering. There was nothing to do but leave it behind and entrust it to the care of an Indian.

The place itself consisted of only five or six bamboo shacks inhabited by Indians, to whom we had the greatest difficulty making ourselves understood. We finally agreed that he was to take care of the horse for about a month, when I would return and would pay him 2 piaster for his trouble. I felt that only the man's honesty would keep him from selling the horse and saying that it had died. But I had no other choice and need breaks all laws. The place, as mentioned, consisted of only a few shacks; there was no grass close by, and we gave them only a little corn for the animals. They assured us that we would be in Asonte before sunset, and we decided to get going, although it was threatening to rain. We had now arrived at the river Cauada [Kanjada], which meanders between high mountains and, at this time of the year, is almost dry. The road thus goes through the river bed, which the other and longer road traverses some one hundred and forty times, but now only fifty. This river bed consists of round loose rocks of various sizes over which the poor animals must vault. They continually slide off the rock on which they stepped, and they suffer terribly and can only move very slowly forward. The blacksmith in Chicontepec had only shod two of my animals, one of them belonged to my Mexican and the other was the one my Portuguese was to ride. When that horse turned out to be too hard for him, they traded, and that was the one which became lame, since it had already lost one shoe. My own horse got such sore feet that it was almost impossible to get it out on the stones, and I believe that I suffered more than it did, since I worried that it would collapse with me on the road. It now started to rain and the footpath, which had been visible as a white strip of rocks caused by them rubbing together, and what had fallen from the animals, became almost invisible. It was also getting towards evening, and there was neither house nor fire to be seen. I had not counted on the unfortunate stones, as little as on the distance, and, when it became completely dark and the rain increased violently, I must admit that I felt very uncomfortable. Continuing was completely impossible, since we were unable to see the path or where we were to cross the river. We thus had no other choice than to spend the long night on the rocks, getting ourselves and our gear soaked, and what was even worse, leaving our brave animals without any feed.

I was conferring with my Portuguese about whether we should stay in the middle of the river or go to the bank under the overhanging trees when he noticed a donkey, loose and alone, close by. He knew from experience that they are seldom far from their masters, and that gave us the courage to keep trying. It was not long before we noticed a small rise in the stones, under which my companion assured me that the donkey's master must lie. He yelled and finally got the answer that there was a house close by. But since it was impossible for us to find our way there in the darkness and I promised a rich reward for the effort, a man rose up from the riverbed and offered to show us the way. He did not think it was possible to get up the bank with the animals, so I then sent the Mexican with the man and waited for their return on my poor Rosinante. Finally, when the water was streaming down my neck through my straw hat, they returned, accompanied by two Indians with torches, or rather, blazes of pinewood. They led us through a thicket and some kind of plantation to a shed that was used for cooking sugar, and outside was a press in the most natural condition. These good people did not understand a word of Spanish but were able to tell us how much we had to pay them, which was only insignificant compared to the service they had provided us. We cut some sugar canes, got a few bananas, and with that and what was in my box, we had a wonderful evening meal and a rest, which was not interrupted until morning, although I then noticed that water had come through the roof and I would not have been protected from it if it had not quit raining.

The morning was one of the most enjoyable in this wonderful climate. The rising sun illuminated the mountain peaks around us and left a vivid reflection on the broad and light green banana leaves with dew and raindrops on their tips. My poor animals, who had not had a single kernel during the night, behaved pitifully when they again had to go out and balance on the terrible stones. In order to ease the burden on my horse, I walked ahead, but I must admit that every moment I expected to be told that one or the other of the animals had collapsed or gone lame. This fear robbed me of the joy I would otherwise have had of the exalted beauties of nature on all sides of us: enormous mountains partly covered with the tallest trees, sometimes so steep that the naked rock wall appeared in the most wonderful and regular stone layers of various natures and colors. Numerous, variously colored birds filled the air with screech and song and flew from one tree or bush to another, which were just as varied in type and color as they. From time to time, there were songs and calls from Indians, many of whom were going to town to celebrate Easter, and some with their baskets on their backs walked to the capital to sell the products of their industry and bring back their few necessities of European origin. We sometimes met whole groups of all ages and genders sitting on the banks of a stream to eat their primitive meal of coconuts and other fruits and some tortillas, and several times, we saw that the women took advantage of this rest period to wash their clothes and take a bath at a remote spot, but completely in their birthday suit. Since many of them are very shapely, I must admit that out of fear of an expression of the well-known Indian jealousy, I avoided taking a second look at them.

Without the loss of anything other than my spurs, which broke on the rocks, we arrived in Asonte at about ten o'clock. This is a church town of about 6-800 inhabitants, and we had the satisfaction of finding adequate feed of all kinds for my brave animals. Since I considered it impossible that the road could be any worse than the part we had already traveled, I considered continuing after having fed the horses, but I received some contrary information. They assured me that the road from now on would be bad and advised me not to attempt to climb the mountains until the next morning, partly for the sake of my animals, and partly because I would not be able to reach any houses before nightfall. A man who had recently returned from Mexico City consoled me by telling that the road up higher was very unstable in several places, and that during his fourteen days there, seven travelers had been killed by robbers. Having once decided to finish what I had started, this information made me more cautious, but it did not put my mind at ease, and it had already been adversely affected by the difficulties I had experienced.

To this, we could add the prospects for the next day, which had been described so darkly to me, and some difficulty with a drunk Indian, who urged me to leave the place where I had arranged for lodging and to go to a different house, which he assured me was the town inn. When I did not want to give in, he gathered a flock of his drinking partners around me. They started screaming and yelling, but I understood very little of it, and, when I discovered that my men were cowards who did not want to get mixed up in the brawl, I strapped on my pistols and took my rifle and explained as well as I could that the first one who touched my belongings, which they wanted to drag over to the other house, would get a bullet in his stomach. They appeared to understand this perfectly and, one by one, they disappeared. However, I was unable to suppress an unpleasant feeling, which was natural after what I had heard and knew about the vindictiveness of these people. It was from a very nice woman, at least in appearance, where we had spent the day, and she had treated us to the best she and the town were capable of. But when evening came, she showed her virtue in an even nicer light by assuring us that, as a woman alone, she was unable to take us into her house, which had only one room. Her brother told us later that her modesty was a result of the jealousy of a drunken husband, who would not hesitate to mistreat her when, upon his return from Mexico City, he found out that she had permitted strange men to spend the night under his roof. The nice woman talked an old neighbor into moving out of his house, which was built from reeds placed side by side in the ground and tied together in the middle, but without any chinking, so that one was able to see through the house. It was not long before I noticed a whole swarm of people; they had been gaping at me all day and still had not gotten their fill but had to inspect my bed through the wall.

I was not convinced, after the scene I had witnessed earlier, that it was just curiosity which drew my observers; so I took the liberty of dousing the light after having placed my rifle and a saber against the bed and placing my pistols under the head of the bed. In passing, I must mention that I had not thought about loading the rifle. My host's furnishings, consisting of a cow hide, which served as a mattress, an old cape, a clay pot and a water ewer, were moved out, and he returned several times to make sure that nothing had been forgotten.

Four posts in the ground and covered with some rough boards and serving as a bed, table and bench, on which the cow hide had been placed, he was gallant enough to leave to my Portuguese, who found it to be a wonderful resting place, while the Mexican rested his lazy body on the floor, which was just clay on which he had placed the horse blankets. He was wrapped up in his old silver-braided cape with velvet trimmings, and his saddle served as his pillow. There was no evil in this kind fool, and, since he had started his career as a houseboy in St. Louis, where he had a rich uncle, he had to show his good manners by talking to everyone who he had barely met and telling everything he knew and did not know about me, and about all of his experiences, which he always began with his rich uncle in St. Louis. His braided cape and immense laziness were probably leftovers from his former dignity, but the former clashed with his other clothing, where elbows stuck out through both shirt and blouse. The piece between the upper and lower piece of clothing was a black rag, which is easy to understand when one knows that he did not change even once on the two-week trip and did not shave off his black beard or wash his face or his hands. But, here, honesty and loyalty is the most important thing, and I had every reason to believe that possessed both.

We spent a quiet night, although I woke up many times, worrying about oversleeping, since I knew that my people would sleep till noon if I did not wake them up. Shortly after sunup, we had the animals ready and began our day's journey, which started with our last crossing of the "Kanjaden," after which we immediately started towards the mountains. The town of Asonte lies in a valley surrounded by high forest-covered mountains and looks absolutely beautiful from above. The road was very steep and, in many places, had many sharp stones, which were the ends of the rock layers, which are like roof tiles. My horse had more difficulty walking than previously, and, since its back was also being rubbed raw by the saddle, I got off and walked and my people followed my example. My poor horse walked to the side several times and finally laid down, a sure sign of illness. It had cost me 80 piaster, but this was a pittance compared to the difficulties in getting another to replace it, and I must admit that it made me feel bad. When it appeared that it was going to collapse, I had the saddle removed, and immediately, it got back up and seemed as satisfied as before.

My Mexican fool had tightened the girth too much under it, and that was what made it sick. I was relieved, and I needed that to face what was coming. The road became worse and worse, extremely steep in places so that the animals could hardly climb. What was even worse was that in other places the rocks were so far apart going down that they had to drop their front legs with the entire weight of the animals on the sharp and pointed rocks, not loose but exposed ends of the rock as mentioned above. I had thought the previous day that nothing could be worse for the horses than the loose rocks in the "Kanjaden," but now I learned something completely different. It was often impossible to get my poor, sore-footed horse to move without driving it hard from behind, leading it by a long rope. Soon, its hooves started to split and bleed. I also got very tired from jumping from one rock to the next, soon up and then down while pulling my horse in the hot sun, which luckily enough was hidden by the shade of the trees which covered the mountain. It was not long, however, before the road which I had found to be so bad, which it truly was, seemed more desirable to me. Hardly had we reached the top of the mountain whose ridge we were to follow, before, instead of rocks, we had clay with deep holes filled with water into which the animals had to step, and a small rise between each from which the horses would slide every time they placed their feet on it. While I was able to walk on the rises, the horses had to step in the holes of the one in front, and they were so deep that they sank in almost to their bellies, and finally appeared to become very depressed. In some places, the road was completely dissolved, and then I had to wade through mud above my ankles. But my suffering was nothing compared to seeing the poor animals dragging themselves along, and, among them, a mule carrying about 150 pounds.

If I had previously feared that I might lose one of them, then I must admit that it seemed now a miracle that I would be able to keep even one of them. I do not believe that I have ever felt worse, since if even two of them had collapsed, or just my pack animal, I would have forced to stay on the road until someone else had showed up. How would I ever get someone else? We were many miles from a living soul, and even farther from anyone who could sell us any pack animals. Even in Asonte, it was uncertain that we could find any. And, if we found one, would I have enough money to meet the exaggerated demand that my dilemma — the dilemma of a foreigner — no doubt would call for? No one in Tampico had prepared me for anything like this, and, in order not to lose too much in case I got robbed, I had only brought along about double of what my travel expenses could amount to. If I ran out of money, I would either have had to give up some of my clothes, if suggested, or if not, send one of my people to Tampico or Mexico City and then wait at least a week for his return. In the meantime, I was on a mountain ridge in a large forest without a roof for miles, exposed to industrious Mexicans' nightly industry. I cannot deny that I dreaded that thought, and my mood worsened when I asked my Portuguese, from whose experience I could expect advice, what could be done in such circumstances. He answered me, "Do what you want, you are the master." That was his usual reply, although he seldom was satisfied when I told him my opinion.

I must admit that my fingers itched to box his ear, but I had second thoughts, since this was hardly the best way to secure good advice, and I was better served with a bad adviser than no one at all. After toiling for six hours, we gave ourselves and our four-legged stable-fellows an hour's rest, took out our provision box, and then continued our journey. We were refreshed, although we were still ignorant about the end of our difficulties. After about an hour, the road got better, and I had an opportunity to admire the wonderful nature all around me. All around were high mountains and deep valleys with dense forests between them. Among them were trees of a height and girth I have never before seen, but in the distance, they looked like shrubbery. Below us were many clouds in strange shapes, and sometimes we were completely enveloped by their fog. The road was like a sick person, who is slowly improving, with relapses but less severe for each repetition. I continued the trip on foot, and we arrived tired at sunset in a small village, where we took lodging. The surroundings were especially charming with the path going along the side of the mountain, and there were several fields with corn, sugarcane, plane-trees and some cotton, with Indian huts in between the bushes. There was an extraordinarily wide view, since the mountains were separated, forming spaces of varied depth and width, until, in the distance, other mountains formed in their center.

In the house where we stayed in Calacatipan, we found plenty of corn for the animals and eggs, frijoles and tortillas for ourselves. A beautiful girl about 15 or 16 years old was squatting down grinding the corn while the mother patted the dough between her hands to form cakes and then baked them, squatting by the fire, which as usual was no higher than the floor. Several, pretty children stood around gawking at me, but I soon got them busy chasing away pigs and poultry from the horses' corn, which they had to eat off the ground, where it was placed on a blanket, since they had no stables or mangers. The master of the house arrived shortly, but no matter how nice the other family members were, he appeared to be able to be up to anything, and I did not forget to take my usual precautions when he showed me to my sleeping quarters — a chicken coop on stilts. I had to enter it on a long pole with steps carved into it, and absolutely matched the origin and usual purpose of the bedroom. The wind on the high mountain was very cold and so strong that my stick house creaked and shook, and the curtain above my bed was so full that I feared that it would pull the house down and bury me under the ruins.

The rain that had threatened the previous night had passed over, and that was just as well, since open walls and a roof with natural air holes was to me not the best kind of shelter, although a hen and maybe two would have been able to find shelter from the soaking. My host, whom I had judged to be dishonest, proved by his bill that he was capable of doing much, and later by stealing a… [sic], which my Portuguese had not watched closely enough, showed that he had talent for even more. Happy to have gotten away that easy, we continued the next morning hoping against all hope, no matter how often I had been fooled, that my host's assurance that the road was good, would be true. This only happened after a half day's travel and when we could see the town of Guaya, which was beautifully located on a mesa formed by lower mountains in the shape of a semi-circle with a deep wooded valley on all sides except for a tongue where the road crossed.

After we had left Calacatipan, I assumed that we would be going down, since we had already climbed considerably. This was a miscalculation, as were so many others, and, for several hours, we kept climbing until we came to a short pass at the highest peak, maybe 10,000 feet, where the view was absolutely gorgeous. The highest mountains, which we had been able to see for several days, and some of which had strange shapes, were now close and even higher than where we were. Many had dark bare summits, but most of them were wood-covered, so that only naked rock walls showed up between the green. Here and there, we saw smoke in the mountains, and a few Indian shacks and halfway tilled fields were witnesses that a few humans took advantage of a natural setting, the richness of which only appeared to be for the rough inhabitants of the air and the forests. I soon felt that no matter how tiresome nature seems when everything bears the sign of human hands and art, wilderness is even more tiresome without signs of human existence. The road seemed, in many places, to be very dangerous, and a misstep by the loyal animals could have sent me to eternity. Yet, I have to admit that after the description I have often heard, I had imagined that the paths would be even more dangerous. It was possible to avoid the danger, if not for the animals then for oneself, by getting off and walking.

We saw Guaya several hours before we reached it, along a beautiful road on the side of the mountain across from and around the town and with a deep valley between. Since we had nothing to do there, and the road led outside the tongue of land leading to it, I sent the Portuguese in to ask for directions to our destination. He did such a good job that the path we, or rather I, took, since I was always in the lead, took us several miles into the forest and finally into a valley, where the road ended, and all around us were high mountains. We got off our horses and followed the sound of a wood cutter up in the mountains. He did not hear our shouting until we were within firing range. We then found out that we were to return the way we had come. With the promise of a tip, he said he would show us a shortcut if we would wait until he came. We returned to our horses, but whether his promise was given to fool us or he had regrets about it, he just started cutting wood again and left us yelling and screaming. Fortunately, our desire to do such vocal exercises was not any greater than waiting in this place with the daylight fading. On our own, we started the return trip after having lost almost two hours. My annoyance increased when nobody of the people we met was able to tell us where San Josef Uchico was located. This was the next place in my directory. They did point us to a different name, San Yago, and the road was good, but did become more rocky, and the soil less fertile as we advanced. The trees did not look as healthy, and there were naked mountains in the distance. While nature had smiled at me, I had no thoughts of evil people, but as soon as the scenery around me changed and the night, which comes suddenly at these latitudes after sunset, my thoughts came back to stories I had heard about attacks, and I wished for signs of a house, for which we had been searching in vain for a long time.

Involuntarily, I checked to see if the powder was all right in my pistols, since we were passing one of the dark canyons that Walter Scott describes so well and which seem to be an ideal place for a Rinaldo of Mexican race to ply his trade. I admitted to myself that this would probably be the worst place on the whole trip to spend the night since there was nothing for the horses to eat, all the grass was scorched by the sun, and the fields were covered with sharp stones which would be difficult for the animals to walk over. There were also just a few sad-looking trees, which would not provide any kind of shelter in case of rain, or against two- or four-legged enemies. It was hard to see the road, and I thought how lucky we had been in "Kanjaden," when we, or rather my Portuguese — because I could not see anything — noticed the roof of a shack a little ways off, and we rushed to it. With much difficulty, we did reach a low shack, which was so full of people, children and animals that it was impossible to consider spending the night there. There was no corn or grass for the animals, and I was already beginning to express my impatience when we were told that there was a better house nearby, and a young man led us to it. To our satisfaction, we found it to be a new and unoccupied house that my Portuguese's seafaring eyes had discerned in the dark and where we could spend the night. There was plenty of corn, and a nice old lady lived in a shack next door, alone with her cat and some poultry. She was willing to prepare for us anything she had in the house. I left it up to my two companions, and held on to my box and a cup of chocolate, which my hostess had prepared.

The next day brought on new trials, which, if my lucky stars had not been watching over me, could have been very serious. In leaving, I inquired as usual about the condition of the road, and if there were many rocks, which I feared more than anything else, although I was riding a mule and letting my horse take it easy. Our kind hostess assured me that, except for a few rocks at the beginning, the road was quite good. However, before we had proceeded 200 paces, it turned out that the road crossed a rocky gulch, or *barricara*, filled with the most terrible rocks and almost vertical walls of a height of perhaps 1,000 feet up and down. Here, I again had to dismount and walk on that terrible road, and it took almost 2½ hours in an intolerable heat of the sun. So far everything was all right, but we had hardly reached the other side, where the road was level and very good, before my loyal *cacho de cargo* [the mule that carried the cargo], started acting pathetically. It would lie down every few moments and try to roll over. I had them remove the load, thinking that it was hurting the animal, but we had hardly tied it on again before it began again, and it was easy to see that the poor animal had some internal discomfort. The mules always go unhitched with their load, but when mine kept going off the path and galloping off and then lying down, I led it by the halter; things went well for some distance until it finally threw itself down, hit its head against the ground and appeared to be about to die.

Fortunately, we were near a village with a large *hacienda*, or farm, where there would be hope for getting a replacement in case it died. I felt so sorry for the poor animal, which had served me so faithfully this long way, that I could have lain down beside it and comforted it. But my servants had a different idea about the way to get it to move. Both of them started beating it with all their strength, and the poor sinner dragged itself up to the farm, where they removed the load. Several donkey drovers were there at that time, and they told me immediately what the poor animal needed, and that they would cure it in an instant. They took it to a deep pond, where they washed it all over, and then rode it full speed through the farm yard, whipping it terribly. The result was that the animal passed its water, and that was what it needed; if it had not been caught in time it could have died. If this had happened to me — not in the mountains, but anywhere else, I would have been most embarrassed, and I have already mentioned earlier, how it would have seemed to me if it had happened in the mountains. That was probably the only place on the long journey where such an occurrence as the one with the donkey drovers would not have had unpleasant consequences for me, something I really can appreciate.

While they were occupied with the animal, a man came down from the residence and invited me to come in. Three gentlemen greeted me and asked where I came from and where I was going, and if I had any news. When they learned that I was a foreigner, they asked many strange questions which I, partly because of my limited knowledge of Spanish and partly because they were unbelievably absurd, had difficulty answering. Finally, they invited me to have dinner with them, and I gladly accepted. The party consisted of the three men and me. One of them was the priest from a neighboring town; because of the holidays he had come to perform services in a small church near the farm, since they did not have a priest. His questions kept me on my toes. The other two were the manager of the farm and his brother, two young men aged 25 to 30 years. I had to tell them where I came from (I said France, since I would be unable to explain to them where Denmark was located). They also wanted to know if France was not a subject of Spain and if it was ruled by an emperor or a king, and if Napoleon had returned, as well as many other questions of that caliber, to which I enjoyed giving them as truthful an answer as possible. Our meal was not bad and even the tortillas were so thin and well baked that I ate them with relish.

After the meal, I had a cup of excellent chocolate with the obligatory glass of water as a chaser. This is so pleasant after the chocolate that it is said that the Spaniards often drink it in order to enjoy the water even more. They then took me around to see the farm, where they only raised the crops needed to feed the great number of horses and mules, the sale of which made up its income. The fields around were quite scorched by the drought and heat, and only in the shrubbery for several miles were the animals able to find something to eat. Only the breeding donkeys and mares were at the farm. The building was a two-story one, made of stone, and had windows and a large cross on the wall. This would probably indicate that it was built to be used as a monastery or had served as the residence of a prelate, which seems reasonable since the church was adjacent to the main building.

The church door appeared to stand open all the time, and since the altar was right in the middle, everyone had to remove their hats every time they passed. I was irreverent enough to ignore it. Behind the farm was a small kitchen garden with a few fruit trees, and it was well maintained. Its beautiful green color was a true and pleasant contrast to the fields, which looked exactly like the Copenhagen commons after the harvest. Gardens are rare in Mexico due to the care that is needed to maintain them because the sun burns up all the vegetables and water is scarce during the dry season. Care and cultivation of items which add to the comforts in life are also seldom found in the Mexican lexicons. The high mountains I crossed the last few days are a "Green of Cordilleras," which stretches all the way through America. We were now on a plain, which itself was a mountain, although it did not seem like it with the many sky-high mountains rising in front of us. At the foot of them was *Anatoltonilco et Grande*, a not-so-insignificant town the towers of which we could easily see at a distance we estimated to be three to four miles. My intent was to spend the night there in order to arrive in Real del Monte early the next day. This is a mine operated by an English company, and I had an introduction to its manager. From there was just a two days' trip to Mexico City along an uninterrupted plain. I was told, however, that the road that seemed so straight-forward to Anatoltonilco was cut by a gorge no less than three miles wide, namely, almost one mile down in numerous turns. This was necessary in order to get down an almost vertical rock-wall in order to be able to maneuver, then one mile over, and one mile up. This far from pleasant information, especially with my mule in its current condition and a gathering thunderstorm, moved me to postpone continuation of my trip till the following morning, and I did not regret my decision.

I must here mention a trait in Mexican honesty, and I like to do it since I think such examples are rare. I had turned over some harness to have it repaired by the donkey drovers who had cured my mule. They did a good job, and I was glad to pay them what they demanded: 1 piaster for the harness and two *reales* (¼ piaster) for curing. In the evening, the farm owner came and gave me two *realer*, which he said that his people had overcharged me, and he apologized that they had wanted to take advantage of the presence of a stranger.

I must admit that I was curious about seeing such a gulf, which I could not even imagine, although the opposite side was clearly visible right in front of me, and looked like a surface only broken by a few trees and small hills. I was convinced that no matter how dark this day's travel had been described to me, it could not possibly be worse than what we had already overcome. The enormous *barranca* soon appeared before us, and the sight of its tremendous dimensions became more frightening and beautiful the closer we got to it. In the valley flowed the Rio Grande River, which we would have to wade across, and from here it looked like an insignificant brook. Both banks were covered with the most beautiful green shrubs, which later turned out to be gigantic trees, surrounded by fertile fields of sugar cane, corn and bananas. There were many houses, and cattle were grazing under the trees. The path had many bends and thus became less steep and difficult, but the insufferable sharp rocks forced me to get off the horse. The opposite rock wall was completely vertical, and it was impossible to determine where and how the ascent could begin. It was also completely black and naked and looked terrible. The water in the river reached the bellies of the animals, and they had to continually vault over round boulders as in Kajaden.

There was a long stretch where I continually feared that either my sick Macho or one of the others was going to collapse, but they acted heroically, and I was beginning to hope that they would last till we got to Mexico City. Water was streaming down the rocks from springs on all sides, and we ran into many dams across the road which led the water into the fields, which were looking beautiful. The naked rock wall we were to climb did not look any less frightening up close than it had from a distance, and I could not imagine how we were to conquer it until we were at the top. Close to the end, the path was so steep that it, at times, was necessary to take the loads off the animals, and we had to carry them. I still wonder how my sick mule was able to drag itself up. It is true that several times I was forced to crawl on all fours and that my conviction from the morning that there was no way that this path could be worse than what we had previously experienced in several places evaporated like dew before noon.

We finally had everything at the top of this in every respect so terrible *barranca* [canyon], which was marked by a big cross. In front of us was a wide plateau surrounded by mountain ranges full of silver and gold mines, and behind those was the big plateau where Mexico City is located. To the right, we saw Anatoltonilco, which we passed in order to proceed straight to Real del Monte, which I wanted to reach in order to spend the rest of the day looking at the mines. The plain we were going to ride across was as ugly as anything, poor soil full of rocks and scorched grass and, here and there, a wretched shack without any trees except for the *Nopal* with its thick leaves that grow out of each other and look very melancholic. The roads are beginning to become unsafe at night and many travelers have been robbed even at the farms where they have sought lodging. The road is quite good, and even good enough that we met a very pretty cart pulled by six black mules and the driver and servant dressed in livery, and a man and a lady riding inside. A groom was riding beside it, leading two horses for a lady and a man. The man in the carriage was wearing a gray coat with braids, and this made me think that it was perhaps General Santa Anna or the deposed President Guerrero himself, whom I, a short time earlier, had been told was staying in the mountains close by, where he had placed several villages under 'contribution.'

At the base of the mountain where we would soon arrive, was a small village showing signs of decay. Several deserted buildings which one could see had been used for cleaning metals made me think that the English company had moved its operations somewhere else. A very wide and excellent drive now led up the mountain and in order to build it, it had been necessary to build bridges from one mountain to another, and at other places, to blast out the rocks and build dams along the sides. This road, which must have been very expensive, was, with all its turns, almost ¾ miles long and offered some great vistas its entire length. As we got up higher, we saw projects that had reference to the mountain works, steam engines that pumped water out of the shafts and big water wheels set into motion by this water, and by intricate connections of several thousand feet in distance, other machinery, partly to pump out the water, and partly to raise the gravel. We finally reached the top of the mountain, which is almost 11,000 feet above sea level. There was a very nice, small village with a beautiful church tower and many houses around about on the sides of the mountain. The inhabitants all made a living from the mines or rather from the English company that operates them. The inn here is operated by a Frenchman, but the furnishings are quite Mexican; namely, four walls, a bench and a table.

The English president of the mines lives in a very nice house, which would have been nice even outside Mexico. I did not find him in town, however, but his secretary came to visit me a short time later and told me that the manager and his wife had gone down to Anatoltonilco, where there are hot baths that she took for her health. I soon discovered that the one I had thought was the Mexican was actually Mr. Tindall with his wife. The secretary, Mr. McIntosh, was very friendly and offered to show me around, but it was getting late, and I preferred to wait and do it on my return trip when I expected to have more time. I continued my trip early the next morning in order to be able to get to Mexico City the following evening. This is the only dangerous stretch on the entire trip, and I had been assured in Tampico that in Real del Monte there were always travelers or donkey drovers in whose company I could spend the last two days of travel. But reality again laid waste to all expectations, and I decided to rely on myself and my lucky stars.

The road down was far worse than the one we had climbed up the mountain, but it was a shortcut for pedestrians and beasts of burden. A better one for wagons was a couple of miles farther on. The road was so steep and full of sharp rocks that I once again had to walk, but that would be the last time on this trip. We were now on the large plateau where the capital is located, but as always, the mountains obstructed the view so completely that it continually seemed as if we were closed in by them and would not get through without climbing them. But as we got closer we could see that they were many miles away and that the plateau ahead of us was immeasurable. It appeared to us as if large lakes surrounded us, and since I was unfamiliar with the landscape, I did not doubt for a moment that it was real. I looked forward to being able to give my animals some water, since my stupid Mexican had forgotten to do that in the morning. This also became a fantasy, and the water disappeared when the mountains retreated as we approached. The only vegetation we saw were *nopale* and aloe, both in different varieties, but as decorative as these strange plants appear among many other trees, just as miserable are they when they stand alone. To begin with, we passed many well-built farms and some sod huts, thatched with wide aloe leaves. Later on, we saw only some buildings and churches in the distance up the mountain side, which, instead of being covered with forest as earlier, were all naked and black just like the rest of Mexico. As plentiful as firewood and lumber are between Tampico and Real del Monte, where all houses were built of wood, just as scarce it is now, and thus all houses are built of dirt or sod and thatched with unbaked bricks and leaves when the owners are unable to build them of stone or wood. This happened so infrequently that the villages a mile distant from the capital, with the exception of one or two buildings in each, were alike.

After having covered a couple of miles, my observations were all of a sudden interrupted by the sad information that my mule again was ill. This necessitated that we again unloaded it. At a shack nearby, we had a bowl made, which we used to bathe the animal from a puddle in the road, and continued our trip after having lost almost an hour. The relief was short, since after about a half hour, the animal again lay down, and only with much difficulty did we it get it to a farm where we hoped to be able to buy another one. But neither there nor at any other place in the vicinity were we able to find a mule for sale, and I considered sending my Portuguese back to Real del Monte and quietly waiting for his return, which would probably take an entire day. Uninformed as I was about what kind of people I had contacted, this could be a very unpleasant situation for me. I thus decided to make another attempt to see if I could find something farther on, which would also take longer. So, after feeding the animal and losing another hour and a half, we loaded up again and continued our trip. Things seemed to go better, and at about three o'clock, we were on a wide plateau which my people told me would be very dangerous because of robbers. There were some beautiful churches and houses on the left side, although far away, and grazing horses and donkeys all around us. My *Macho* again got ill and kept lying down, and was finally hard to move. There was nothing to do but to remove the load - which by the way is a difficult job, especially the lashing - and decide what might be done. As usual, the entire council consisted of my person alone, since my Mr. Portuguese as usual answered: "You are the master and you decide," and the Mexican was too stupid an animal to give one a rational answer. In order to keep their courage up, I gave them what was left of my food while I thought it over: it was impossible to send a message to Real del Monte from where we were, without shelter and with evening approaching and a thunderstorm gathering, in an open field alone with the biggest coward I have ever known, whose weapon consisted of a saber *without a blade*, which he had been conned into buying in Tampico for the same price he would have had to pay for a good one. To go to the closest house would apparently be as useless as it was inadvisable. Only in the towns and on the larger farms can one expect to find mules that are broken in, and if the inhabitants here were villains, it would not be advisable to reveal to them that we had to spend the night in an open field. The final decision was, therefore, after some conflict but *without a scuffle* to try Macho once more and try to reach the first town before nightfall.

In all the time we had hesitated here, we had not seen a single person on the road and thus no robbers either, and for this, we may be able to thank a strong north wind, which the Mexicans cannot stand. It is possible that it is dangerous; I am unable to judge about that. But one thing is sure, that I did not feel a bit uneasy about it, and would have been able to face it with composure. We loaded Macho again and had the joy of watching him not only walk, but even trot, until after a couple of hours, and by nightfall, we reached the village of San Mateo. We had hardly unloaded before the weather we had feared erupted with all force and thunder, more violent than I have ever seen or heard. We learned here that a short time earlier a band of no fewer than sixty robbers on horseback had come into a nearby village with drums and pipes and had stripped it completely. They then disappeared into the mountains where a *Conde* (count) *de Regla* was on their tracks with several troops. As a consequence of this, it was now much safer, but they were still worried about having such a visit later. After this information, I was not unhappy to see a donkey drover arrive later that evening. He was scheduled to be in Mexico City the following evening, and we would be able to travel with him. It also pleased me because of the condition of my mule; if it should fall, I could possibly for a reasonable sum get him to distribute my belongings on his donkeys, and I could thus avoid any embarrassment. We started out before daybreak the following morning, facing an unusually long day's trip, but the road was good and the weather was cool and pleasant. Our traveling companion's flock consisted of sixteen large and small donkeys, all loaded with barley relative to their strength, and even a year-old colt patiently carried its small bag on its back. The drovers, a father and son, dressed in a brown leather jackets and short knee pants, but without buttons or any other kind of clothing under or over, a pair of sandals on their feet and an old straw hats on their heads. They took turns riding a small gaunt nag while the other one continually ran from one donkey to the other to straighten the loads, which shifted constantly since the donkeys could not tolerate that they be tightened as much as on the mules, where it gets cinched so hard that one should think they were made of rock or wood.

Although this was hard work for the men and the animals were carrying heavy loads, they continued right on to Mexico City without taking a rest, while we stopped in a small village to tend to ourselves and our animals. We passed close by a church, where there was music and song, or rather bellowing. I asked about the occasion and was told that it was in honor of a saint, who had recently appeared before them. I naturally found it very praiseworthy that the believers celebrated such an occurrence and was going to the church to see how they behaved when a long train came out in a procession carrying a wooden picture dressed like a monk on a scaffold with a canopy over it. They were screaming loudly to a *charivari* of all kinds, and playing the rawest instruments. All of the observers went naturally onto their knees in the dirt, and it was only by running off that I escaped. Thinking that they would be walking around the town and then returning to the church, we continued our trip after finishing our meal, but we were very surprised to see the procession moving at a snail's pace in the same direction as we did. If we hoped to reach town before evening, we could not afford to lose any time, but my people assured me that it could have serious consequences if we tried to pass the procession. I asked someone along the road how far they were going, and they pointed out a church about a mile away that could only be reached by this road, which was also the road to Mexico City. At the pace they were moving, it would take at least three hours before they reached the church. This is not to mention the intolerable part of crawling behind the procession and having to listen to their bellowing, and it would also be impossible for us to hope to get to Mexico City before nightfall. I thus decided to get around them by crossing across a field and moving fast enough that they would not consider chasing us. After a good deal of objections, especially from my Mexican, I convinced them to follow me as fast as the animals could move. With hat in hand — I just raised mine a little bit from my head — we passed them at a distance of fifty to sixty paces without the least resistance or remark. My macho was wise enough not to lie down after we got back on the road; we would have been quite embarrassed if he had done so.

It is only by the increasing number of beautiful churches that one can see that the capital is closer, since the houses are the same miserable shacks built of clay and thatched with straw or leaves or built of sod to the top without chimney or other air-hole than the door. There are some exceptions where one sees houses built of stone and with a flat roof, which does not really give a more cheerful impression. These shacks cannot be seen from a distance, and it is surprising to see the many magnificent churches without any congregation to attend them. But even taking all of the inhabitants and their misery into consideration, it is easy to see how much the monks have acted as masters over the people and robbed them, just as they burned the first inhabitants: "*tout au salut de leurs amis*" [all to the salvation of their friends]. They are still ruling with the darkest superstition in which they keep the people, and one does not see one person of the lower class, be it man or woman, boy or girl, who does not wear a Paternoster band around his or her neck. Without it, they believe that they would be victims of all sorts of evil spirits. We saw numerous crosses with piles of rocks under them along the road. The traveler learns that where a cross has been erected a person who has been killed has been found and buried, and a believer does not pass it without throwing a rock on the pile. This is to be understood to be an aid for the dead person for getting through Purgatory!

The fields were tilled here, although the soil was poor and there is almost only aloe in them. This plant gives a double, very basic and useful yield. From the sap is prepared *pulque*, the main drink of the people; it is similar to whey both in flavor and appearance, and I find it highly repugnant. From the leaves is extruded a sort of hemp, much stronger than the common kind, and from this all of their ropes are made. Their famous lassos are made from this, and the South Americans use those to catch wild horses and oxen. The Mexicans use them on tame ones, who are so used to the lasso that even the most tired and patient creature does not want to get caught unless it feels the rope around its neck, but then even the wildest one stands still without the least resistance. The lasso is not used on animals alone. Robbers use it as a terrible attack weapon, which I feared more than both rifle and saber. At a distance of twenty to thirty paces and at full speed, they were able to throw the rope with unbelievable skill, and were able to place the noose on any limb of a rider or the horse. By this, either the animal is brought down or the rider is pulled off and dragged over rocks and boulders until he is mutilated, and this terrible death has become the lot of many travelers. The many stories we had heard about robberies had the greatest influence on my Mexican, although he himself looked more like a robber than all of the ones we met and who frightened him very much. At one time, it was a lasso, later an unusually long saber, then a couple of perhaps empty pistol cartridges on a passing horse that turned them into robbers in his eyes and made him tremble like an aspen leaf. He would have been a great help if we had been attacked!

We could finally see the Mexico City at a distance of almost two miles with its numerous towers and domes, but the setting sun behind it and the high dark mountains which seemed to be touching it made it difficult to distinguish the details. Far to the left was the back of a volcano, the top of which was covered with snow and now wrapped in threatening thunderclouds. To the left were lower, green mountains at the base of which the road led, and around a corner with a cross, where all travelers crossed themselves and removed their hats, we saw the town of Nuestra Senora de Guadalupe in front of us, a half mile from the capital. This hamlet, the birthplace of the patron saint of Mexico, appears strewn with churches and monasteries. The cathedral is the richest in the republic; its silver and gold chalices, which are in public view on great holidays, are of immense value, and so far the government has not dared touch them. The picture of the patron saint is adorned with precious stones from head to foot.

From the gate of the town, an avenue leads up to the city; at this time of the year it is pretty good, but it is impassable during the rainy season, when almost the entire area is under water. The Spaniards have erected a stone dam at a great expense across which the road goes. Each side is enclosed with a rock parapet and decorated at regular intervals by flat stone pillars, about fifteen feet tall and six feet wide, into which are carved images of saints and scenes from the Bible, and on top are Mary and the infant. At the Guadalupe's gate was a guard who did not let us pass without a "*licencia de armas*," or permit to carry arms, and I had to go to "*alcalden*" [the mayor— transl.] to obtain mine. The honorable person in charge agreed with me that it was unreasonable and sent his assistant to the guard to lift the embargo placed on us. Meanwhile, the thunder had arrived and the rain poured down, and in order to avoid getting soaked we took refuge in the guard house, where I talked with the sentry. He told me that he was a member of the reserve army from Jalapa, which had overthrown Guerrero, the last president, and that things were now going to be different, because *he* and *his* now were in charge. It appeared, however, as if this very important Mexican hero was not really too happy with some of the new precautions made by *his* new government. Presumably his pay had been delayed, which is the ultimate thermometer of the feelings of these patriots.

Mexico City

Due to this delay, we did not get to Mexico City until after dark, and we were thoroughly searched when entering its gate, since there were both State and City customs. Even on gold and silver coins there was a 2 percent duty, although they came from Mexican mines. When we rode into town, we were told that after "*la oración*" — the six o'clock prayer — it was not permitted to *ride* through the city, and my Mexican immediately got off his horse. I did not let that worry me and that was just as well since we had over a quarter of a mile to go before reaching our inn, and nobody said a word. It appears that this intolerable rule was ecclesiastical, and one is gradually getting wise enough not to blindly obey it. The pavement was of such pointed stones that my sore-hoofed animals had difficulty moving, and a row of tiles in the center of the street was so uneven that they kept sliding when they stepped on them, and that was even worse.

We finally reached the inn in Calle Espíritu [The Street of the Holy Ghost], and I was pleasantly surprised by the appearance of the interior of the courtyard, which was a complete square surrounded by two-story buildings with an overhang resting on posts on three sides and a wide stairway across from the entrance gate in the rear wing, so that one had to walk across the courtyard to get up into the building. This is also the way the large buildings look in Copenhagen, and many of them are prettier, with statues and flower pots with the most beautiful plants on the railings around the gallery. There is carpeting, painted canvas, or just an imitation on the wide stairs, which are made of rocks just like the buildings, and of which from the street through the gateway one can only see the lowest flight. The wall straight across from it is decorated with an original or imitation statue of a saint or something similar.

My room is a small den about twenty to twenty-four square feet, separated from my neighbor by a panel which reaches halfway to the ceiling, and above which the light came in, so it was not exactly dazzling. The host, Hr. Pauli, was a *"brabander"* who had served as a courier under Napoleon and after many adventures had landed here and had more indebtedness than fortune. He was married to a young English woman, who probably attracts more customers than does his pub. I have nothing to say against the man, however. He was very kind to me and a half piaster per day for the room, no matter how small it was, is far from expensive in these latitudes.

Mexico City is located at 19° N. 13, and is thus in the warm zone. It was already the capital of the old Indians when Fernando Cortez conquered it in the beginning of the 16th Century, after having been driven back several times and after having committed the biggest atrocities on the unfortunate natives. It is said that the cathedral is located where the castle of the last king, Montezuma, was located. One must wonder that in an age where the European cities were arranged in veritable labyrinths such good taste had the front seat in the establishment of Mexico City — all streets are straight and of a convenient width, almost like Dronningens Tværgade in Copenhagen. The houses are all built of rock due to the frequent earth tremors, which would collapse less stout buildings. Most of them are two stories high, seldom more than three, or two with a mezzanine. The roofs are all flat built with tiles, and there are no chimneys, since they only burn charcoal due to the lack of firewood, and the smoke escapes through a trap-door in the kitchen ceiling or wherever it can. There is no need for heaters in the rooms, since it never gets really cold although the city is at an elevation of 7,000 feet, and I have been assured that only one early winter morning has there been a thin layer of ice on a...[*sic*] on the town square.

All buildings, with a few exceptions, have balconies arranged in different ways, either outside each individual window, or in a row along all of them. In the nicer houses, the ground floor is only intended for the servants, cart-shed and stables. The merchants use it for their offices and storage of their finer merchandise. This story has a very high ceiling, so that the second floor is as high above the ground as in the best buildings in Copenhagen. In some streets, the second floor is built out over the sidewalk and rests on pillars, and in the arcades underneath are small booths built around the pillars where women sit and sell fruit and bread. The buildings are painted in various colors, as in Copenhagen, and if the paint were better maintained, the inner city would look much better; it cannot be denied that it looks better in panorama than in reality.

The nicest looking part of the city is its numerous churches and monasteries, which are well maintained and take up a great part of each street. The church towers are not pointed as ours, but are either big domes covered with tiles in different colors and placed in shapes of crosses, inscriptions and all sorts of shapes, which reflect in the sun just like St. Petersburg's gilded towers, or two similar flat towers side by side (in which the perpetually chiming bells are hanging). This gives the buildings a far better looking symmetry than in our churches. That which contributes to the nice look of the streets are the usually tall windows with big panes, flower containers on the balconies and sometimes on the roofs, images of saints here and there on the walls, illuminated, where believers never pass without removing their hats or making the sign of the cross. It is also a striking sight with the high mountains, the backs of which appear to go clear up to the end of each street although they are many miles away. There is nothing that disappoints one the way the mountains do, and no matter how often I have been fooled, I often had problems explaining reality.

There are many excellent buildings in Mexico City from the time of the Spaniards which are now difficult to maintain. The big square in the center of town had been very beautiful, until it was decided to build a big cube on one side, which stretches almost to the center of the square, and in which are arranged booths, both outside and inside the building. They have been divided into many regular streets. On December 8, 1828, when Guerrero seized the presidency, his robber bands of soldiers streamed in and plundered everything. Since then, more than half of the booths have been closed and grass in growing in the streets and the courtyard. This building disfigures the square terribly, and there is no reason to leave it standing except for the lack of funds. Except for that, this is a regular square; in the middle, close to the north side, is the magnificent cathedral, built of sandstone, a high dome in the center and, on each side of the façade, two square, flat towers decorated with beautiful statues of the apostles, and a small clock in a little dome above the main entrance.

Adjacent to the cathedral is a smaller one, which disrupts the symmetry; it is the old cathedral with the first seminary. The interior of this has a new and extremely splendid altar, whereas the cathedral is so overloaded with gildings, paintings and pictures that the whole gives a completely opposite impression of what was the original intent. Besides this, they had not been satisfied with the numerous altars along the wall besides the main altar, but had erected another one almost in the center of the church, which completely removes the venerable and impressive part of the building itself.

The east side of the square is totally occupied by the castle where the viceroy used to reside, and which now is the seat for the president and both chambers [of government—transl.], the ministries, and so on. The building is not noteworthy in itself except for its size; it is a low, two-story building without symmetry. The inside is divided into two courtyards, surrounded on all sides with archways on both stories, and here are the entrances to the various offices. Both chambers are located in the rear building, with the one of the representatives extending far over the roof, and on its top, is a gilded statue with a staff crowned with the cap of liberty. The inside of both chambers is as tasteful as can be. The one of the diet forms a semicircle and in the middle of it is a virtual throne, which only lacks a crown. From this, the president opens and closes the meetings, and both chambers meet here. The speaker and the secretaries sit beneath the throne and the members on benches as in an amphitheater. On each side, in front of the speaker, is a lectern of mahogany. In front of the throne on the opposite wall is a large picture of Mary with the infant Jesus: *nuestra patrona* [our patron—transl.], as I was told by the senator who was kind enough to show me around. In the arch, behind the deputies, are the seats for the people, just like the loges in a theater, only without any separation except for the pillars that support them. A violent earth tremor about a year ago necessitated walling up the lower story to prevent the entire building from collapsing. The section between the stories is decorated with the names of those who fell for Mexican liberty. The light comes in from above through blue-painted windows, and it looks very nice. The senate meeting room is the same shape, only smaller. Everything here is mahogany, which gives it a darker appearance, and since the president does not come here, the chairs of the speaker and the secretaries are placed toward the center. The president of Mexico resides in the southern wing. At the present time, there is only the vice president, Bustamante, who last December, after *la declaración de Jalapa* [the Declaration of Jalapa—transl.], overthrew President Guerrero.

The audience hall is very beautiful with the walls, chairs and ottomans covered in yellow satin, and a pretty rug on the floor. This hall is so brilliant because it belongs to the sovereign people, who have free admission to it. We saw slung onto these magnificent sofas and chairs all sorts of rabble both with and without their kit, with cigars in their mouths and hats on their heads, continually spitting on the floor and also decorating the rug with ashes and cigar butts. The president's adjutants did not set a good example, and it was quite natural that they followed it. Such contempt for the top person of authority in the state bothered me no end. I mentioned this to a French gentleman who was with me to introduce me to the vice president, and who was a colonel in Mexican service. He laughed, and so did the Mexicans to whom he relayed my remark, and said that it was easy to see that I had not been in a free country for a very long time. I answered him in French that I could tell that he was military, since I had already learned here that only they and the monks have true freedom, at the expense of others. He gave me a sign of applause and did not translate this remark for his neighbors. General Bustamante was ill, so I did not get to see him. Only later did I see him in a coach; he was a tall man with a big beard and an expressive masculine face.

On the south side of the square is a tall building housing the courthouse and institutions dealing with the City and State of Mexico, separate from the government of the Republic of Mexico. Underneath is an archway with all kinds of shopkeepers, the city jail, the merchants' guild, etc. The west side also has an archway with booths, and up higher near the cathedral is a row of old houses built by Fernando Cortes and still belonging to his heirs. In the center of the square, there used to be a statue of King Carlos III on horseback. After the revolution, it was moved into the museum yard. It is metal, plump but very well executed, and is supposed to be a good likeness. The museum, which is located on the fruit market square just south of the castle, is a large granite building where an academy of sciences used to be located, and where a library and everything needed to reactivate it is still to be found. Nothing is missing except the members. The previous ones were almost all Spanish and were expelled a couple of years ago, and it is now filled with only a few monks' limited monastery learning. The museum itself is a very strange collection of leftovers from the past, and it bears a wonderful witness to artistic ingenuity. Many statues of their idols are not only carved in granite, but in the hardest rock, and no one has been able to discover what kinds of tools they have used. The strangest part is that these statues of idols are very similar to the Egyptian ones, which gives those with learning plenty of material for pondering. A very large sacrificial vessel made of granite, in which prisoners of war were killed, is especially noteworthy for the carvings on its edge, which symbolize the ancient Mexicans' conquest of all of their neighbors. Next to the cathedral is still a large, round stone that looks like a millstone on which is carved numerous figures in twelve sections from the center of the stone. The archaeologists have interpreted it to be an almanac or a sort of Egyptian zodiac and only heaven knows for what reason.

Iturbide, during the short period he ruled as Caesar Augustimus the First and Last, did not live in the castle but in a large building that belonged to it. The government in Calle San Francisco distinguishes itself only in the adding of gilding on doors and window sills, since the rooms were to be very plain. It amused me to see on the wall the Spanish coat of arms, which had been crossed out, again becoming visible. To the superstitious Mexicans, this could appear to be a bad omen. Not far from here is a Franciscan monastery, one of the richest in town, and that says a lot. A beautiful church belongs to it, and all in all, it is expansive. A more utilitarian building is the so-called Minesia; built of granite, it is undeniably the most beautiful in the city. Its purpose is the same as that of the magnificent palace of the mining corps in P[*word erased or smeared*], a place where young people are taught mineralogy and what is needed to make use of the mines, which in both countries make up the most important branch of industry for the government. The Spaniards unfortunately did not consider the nature of the soil on which they erected such a massive building. The consequence is that now that it is almost finished after many years of labor the soil is sinking so that a large part of it must be torn down, which no doubt will prevent it from ever being finished. I found there a class of fewer than 20 young people who were studying natural science. They had a nice collection of English physics instruments, but their collection of mineral samples was poor in comparison with what I have seen other places. Pastors and monks were in charge of the instruction here.

Another very large and impressive building is the Palace of the Holy Inquisition, which has been converted into a customs house, and that is fortunate for them, since there is no doubt that in any future financial crisis they will confiscate the extraordinary wealth of the clergy, which luckily enough for the country has so far escaped. Until now, the government has been in the sad hands of those who want to spend it on themselves, rather than for the good of the State, and to suppress the population rather than preparing the road toward happiness and freedom. But enlightenment cannot be expected to move fast in a country like this one, where the clergy still has such an influence on all classes of superstitious people, and if those in power have so far taken care not to take the majority of the clergy's property, it can only be linked to their fear of the lower classes. The schools are already far from being in a bad condition in the country, and Republican principles must sooner or later find their way to the various classes, and the inevitable result will be a renunciation of the clerical yoke that will be as complete as that of the royal yoke. Upon the expulsion of the Spaniards, many monasteries were closed since most of the monks were born in Europe, and that law reached as far as the archbishop, who had to leave the country and has not been replaced. God knows that there are plenty of monks here in Mexico City and they are of all colors. The most common and numerous ones are the Franciscans, Dominicans and Trappists. They can be seen at all times and in every street with their broad brimmed hats on their heads, a cigar in their mouths and the most impudent look on their mugs. I was told that people out in the country never meet a monk without kissing his cassock or his hand; I was fortunate enough to be spared that sight. It is strange that in such an arch-Catholic country the sale of Spanish translations of books in which Church teachings and the Church itself are openly criticized, is permitted freely. The only explanation I can think of is that the clergy is convinced that the population is so absolutely in their power that they do not dare read such books. They should be on the alert, because the first spark in the darkness could ignite something that could not be extinguished, except on their graves and those of their idols.

The saints are true idols, especially to the Indians, because, at the introduction of Christianity by sword and fire, they abandoned *their* icons for the Catholic ones, learned *Ave* and *Credo*, to kneel and to cross themselves, believe in the Pope and his priests, and then they were Christians. But it is not only the church's and the government's affair to keep the descendants of the original natives as uninformed as possible, since if they became aware of their strength, they could easily provide the Spaniards' descendants with an tainted people in all respects and oust their suppressors, just as they had done to the Spaniards themselves. There are four Indians to each *gachopin* (descended from Spanish ancestors). They are, therefore, careful not to let them read anything but Catholic books in the schools. This makes them more dumb than wise, and the Indians are far from being a naturally dull people. An American educator came here a few years ago for his health, and became aware of the Indians and wished to test their abilities. To that purpose, he got in contact with the then president, Victoria, who let him have two orphan boys aged 8 and 10 years. He sent them to his industrial school in the state of Indiana, one of the United States, and he assured me that he had never seen children with a better ease of learning and greater grasp of things. He reported this to the government upon his return here and offered to take up to 300 boys and teach them useful trades, whereby they would be able not only to support themselves, but also become capable teachers of their countrymen. He offered to do this for 60 piasters annually per boy, which is what they cost the government here without learning anything, but this was denied out of fear that the Indians would become too educated. The *gachopines* were right, because the Indians hated them already, and I have a strange example to prove their aptitude. In Tampico, I had an 18-year-old Indian as my servant, who slept in the same house where I stayed, which otherwise stood vacant. He came home in the evening when it got dark, and when I came in, I could always find him occupied by writing and even doing arithmetic. I read what he had written and was highly surprised at finding a good handwriting and verses. When I asked him where he had learned to read, write and do arithmetic, he answered, "In the school in a small village," and that some of the verses were his own. I will take it for what it is worth, but he started to recite so much that after an hour I got tired of listening and naturally was unable to understand everything. I then read what he had written; some were love poems, not of the highest poetic quality, but they were all decent. The rest consisted of a poem about the defeat of the *barradas* the previous year and one against the *gachopines*, where an Indian strongly praises himself and his nation's antiquity and calls the others bloody conquerors whom the Indians' club some day will fell. I ought to have saved those Indian products. But now back to the capital.

I had started to talk about the monastic system and it will be best if I finish my remarks regarding this self-denying class "whose kingdom is not of this world," and who therefore had amassed treasures at the expense of widows and minors "*a la plus grande gloire de Dieu*" [to the great glory of God]. I do not know whether it is to the honor of God or the edification of the church, that almost all of them — regardless of submission to celibacy — have many children. But likely is it that these paragons of virtue hide here under the cover of the cape of the patriot since it is evident that the republic lacks right hands, and they were Mexicans before becoming priests! One must admit that they are no harder against anyone else than themselves. The above-mentioned young Indian told me that he had two children with different women, and no more considered getting married than did the majority of his countrymen. The pious servant of God never declined baptism and indulgence, if only people were able to pay the price, which was not very high, but it was important. Since their religion consists solely of ceremonies and the people never learn to think, it is natural that priests and people appreciate their observances, and they would for nothing in the world be accused of not having religion. Thus, a child who dies without baptism and an older person without the sacraments are considered to have eternally lost their souls, and that is a greater sorrow for the survivors than death itself. Therefore, when a person is found murdered in the street, which often happens, and there is still life left, nobody considers sending for a doctor any more than they consider pursuing the murderer. But *everybody* wants to save his soul, and there is just one call: *el padre, el padre* [the father, that is, the priest, the priest].

The sacrament is the Catholic Church's *Sacrum sanctorum*, but nowhere else do they worship idols in this respect than they do here. Since the restoration in France, a "*le petit bon Dieu*," as they call it, is carried under a canopy to the home of the sick, and one does not need to remove one's hat when it passes by, although the old woman kneel and I have even seen a sentry at his post do it. It is quite different here, where our master rides in a coach with an escort of horsemen in front and behind and two long rows of church servants on both sides, with white cassocks over their clothing and with long staves with lanterns on the end. They shout litanies and are accompanied by a bell carried in front of the procession and sounding incessantly. The coach is pulled by two white or piebald mules and has windows on all sides. It is driven by a high-ranking church official on general occasions, but if it is a military person for whom the sacrament is meant, the wagon is driven by an officer, who rides one of the donkeys and has his cap under his arm, and at each side of the door is a column of officers, likewise with their caps in hand, and soldiers outside of them again. If the sick person is an officer, the *colonel* of the regiment rides as driver, and often the regiment's entire Turkish orchestra marches in front playing the noisiest marches, and with that noise, they go to the dying man. The house, however, is decorated as for a celebration, with flowers strewn in the hall and on the stairs; in the rooms are hung the best blankets of the house, and all relatives of the sick person receive the priest on their knees, and wearing their best. There is no doubt that such a spectacle has killed many ill ones, but that is a trifle if only his *soul* has been saved. As soon as the bell and singing can be heard on the street where the procession is passing, one must remove one's hat, and as soon as it comes into view, one must kneel down and stay in the dirt until it is out of sight, and that can take half an hour in the mile-long streets. Even inside the buildings one must watch out; a few years ago an American was killed in a shop because he failed to kneel, and the American attaché was unable to have the murderer arrested and punished. Even on the balconies, one only dares kneel, and in the evenings, one sees all over lights placed there and women kneeling. During recent years, many of the foreigners who visit here now, without the Mexicans themselves knowing or willing to admit to it, have had a favorable influence on their prejudices and one is far less frequently exposed to rough treatment than a few years ago. I thus avoided not only kneeling, but even removing my hat by rushing away as soon as I heard the bell, which sometimes did not happen until everyone around me was already kneeling. A young Englishman who stayed at the same inn where I did was twice forced to kneel, and one of the times he was on horseback, but had come too close to the procession before he noticed it and was thus immediately stopped. It is difficult to determine how long such intolerable fanaticism will last, and probably neither we nor our children will see a noticeable change. The fact that the entire effort of the clergy revolves around maintaining it and, in doing so, even utilizing the most shameful methods can be shown by the following.

There is a church on one of the mountains near the capital. It is consecrated to Nuestra Señora de Buen Secorro [Our Lady of Perpetual Help], and during Lent, her picture is brought downtown in a big procession that takes two days to covering three miles. People now believe that this picture comes to heal all the sick and those unfortunate people who walk or are carried in the procession, no matter how harmful the air may be to them. Last year, smallpox was rampant in town, and instead of advising that mothers not bring their sick children out or postponing the procession, the priests, who should know better, permitted everyone to follow it on the day it was normally to be, and thus would rather sacrifice the hundreds of innocent people who died from the consequences than tell them the truth. And do not think that the consequences enlightened them; credit is given to the picture for the few who were healed, and they are absolutely convinced that if they had stayed away, everyone would have kicked the bucket.

Mexico City has almost 160,000 inhabitants, of which many are foreigners, especially French, who have come here to make a rich harvest of doubloons and piasters for the negotiables they brought with them, and which were as suitable for the Mexican markets as was rye for those along the Mediterranean. The result was that for each person who managed a passable profit, nine lost everything they had, and in order not to return home as beggars, they remained in the country, occupied with building "castles in Spain" with the rest of their capital, meanwhile blaming their country, people and government for their bad luck. They were careful not to take any blame for their recklessness in the choice of their merchandise and the resulting loss. As far as the people go, God knows that an honest picture is dark enough by nature that one does not need to lie in order to paint it darker still. The lower class here is terrible, and a gentleman who recently arrived from Naples assured me that their appearance was worse than that of its ragamuffins. The Mexican rascals stand around in groups on street corners or lie on the sidewalks dressed in brown skin vests and bared chests and short pants of the same material and an old straw hat on their heads and either without shoes or wearing sandals. It would be impossible to imagine them wearing a shirt. Every other moment there is quarreling going on among these fellows, and it is usually settled with the knife, which everybody carries strapped to their side. You seldom see anyone who does not have deep scars all over their limbs. Their brown faces and black eyes are so full of expression that nobody who has seen them needs to ask if the city is safe, or wonder why every shop is equipped with iron doors and almost a dozen padlocks, one above the other. As far as clothing goes, the higher classes are morally only slightly superior. Hypocrisy embellishes them all and that corrupt faith can only breed corruption.

The gambling disease cannot possibly be seen to be worse than here, and it reigns in all classes in the most terrible manner. Many make a living from this noble business and hundreds of gambling houses are open from early morning till late at night, always filled with people seeking their fortune. Strangers are quickly caught up in this current and thus most of them lose the fruits of their more or less fortunate activities. It is common at the gambling tables to borrow from one's neighbor when one has lost, and that carries on to the outside, and if one is led astray along that path, it is usually difficult to recover what one has lent to someone. One can expect the worse if one presses someone for repayment without legal proof, and even then, one must watch out. Well-dressed people occasionally stop you in the street to borrow money from you, and even the fair sex is very well versed in the art of tricking strangers in particular. I took my meals at a

French lady's house, where several Germans also ate; among them was a watchmaker who had settled in town. One day he came late to dinner and told us that just as he was to leave his shop, two neighbor women, whom he had often seen but never spoken to, came and asked him if he would let them listen to some music. He wound up a clock and let it play and they asked about the price. After it had quit playing, they asked if they could hear another one, until he had played all of them. He thought that they were going to buy something in appreciation for his trouble, but they just sat there until he indicated that he had to leave. One of [them] said that the reason she had come was to ask him to lend her ten piasters. He excused himself by saying that he only had a half, and she responded with a surly: "Oh! Until next time, then!" If he had lent them the money, he would never have seen them or his piasters again, and would have been abused had he asked for repayment.

Since the passion for gambling goes from the president clear down to the most wretched Indian, I do not think there is any hope for improvement unless the people can be inspired to go to work. In order to bring that about, the ones who are able and wish to provide jobs must be assured that their rights to their property are not violated by war or other force, and the many ne'er-do-wells, mainly from the army, must be hindered from doing any harm. As soon as the republic is able to lay down its weapons against foreign enemies, it might be possible to reduce the number of its worst domestic enemies, which undeniably is made up of its soldiers whose minds are naturally directed toward war. If there are no opportunities outside the borders, there may possibly be an opportunity within the borders of a country, where the rights have solely been in the hands of the strongest. The present rulers are already busy with encouraging the establishment of manufacturing plants in the country, and if peace is first secured and faith in the future is possible, there is no doubt that such enterprises would be advantageous to the character and morals of the people. The way it is now there is not a hamlet without public gambling houses, and every Saturday evening, when the lower classes like to get together at a place in town to dance their *fandango*, there are tables placed all over where men and women can try their luck.

Near the capital, there is a village by the name of San Agostino, where the *fiesta*, or festival of saints, which takes place in May, attracts not only half of the population from the capital but additional thousands from many miles away due to its reputation of the treasure placed on the tables there. All these thousands come there to try their luck. There are gaming tables where the stakes are solely in gold and, in just a few hours, rich families have often been ruined. Although, at that time, it is impossible for even the most unscrupulous price to obtain a roof over their head and tortillas for food, it does not discourage prominent ladies from going there, and it can only be compared to the citizens of Copenhagen going to "Dyrehaven" which, thank God, does not have the same purpose. My acquaintances wanted to persuade me to postpone my departure a couple of weeks to be able to take part in this entertainment, about which everyone was talking, and they had a difficult time understanding that I did not want to take this opportunity to get rich quickly.

As mentioned earlier, the people must learn to appreciate the need for more useful and secure ways of earning a living, but this is not going to happen before this madness gets changed. I have also mentioned that although foreigners know a better way of investing their money, they still get caught up in this. The English consul general, who is married to a wealthy Mexican lady, has lost not only his sizable fortune, but also his salary for the next three years! The aforementioned young Englishman who lived at the same inn as I had come to Mexico to pick up his inheritance from his uncle, who had closed the Mexican loan in London and had the most beautiful opportunity of obtaining the most brilliant fortune, had the man of purely English originality not gone half-crazy and not only concerned himself with getting more, but also with effort had tried to finish off what he already had. Fortunately for his heirs, he had kicked the bucket, and this 20-year old nephew, who had never done anything but enjoy himself in London and thus had thought only for dressing up and blowing hot air, now came over to complete a complicated liquidation. Before leaving England for the last time, the uncle had told him that in the wall of his house, under one of the windows, which he described exactly, he had bricked up a treasure of almost 20,000 piasters. He died before he could return to Mexico and the treasure still had to be there.

The first thing our Dandy did after his arrival was to locate the precious place, which he found to be exactly as described, and tear down the wall to secure whatever was in it. However, things went the way they often do for many treasure-hunters. He found a well-arranged gap in the wall just the right size to contain the treasure, but that was all; it was as empty as his brain. He did not settle for that, however. The uncle had probably been wrong about the window and had prepared this gap for a new treasure. He thus worked fast, and one piece of the wall fell after another, with the same luck; the uncle had hidden his treasure so well that there was nothing for our friend to do than pay 4,500 piasters to get the wall rebuilt. Whether it was this enterprise or another no less brilliant one which he undertook in Jalapa — where, out of zeal for Protestantism and to contribute his part to the fall of Catholic idolatry, he one day walked into the church and took a silver crucifix from the altar in front of which he had seen some women kneel. He put it under his clothing and walked out with it — an act which without fail could have cost not only his, but the life of many of his countrymen. It is incomprehensible that this did not happen — that encouraged him to seek new opportunities to show his talent, I shall not say. But it is true that before I left Mexico, he spent at least nine of his day's fourteen hours (he got up at ten o'clock and went to bed at twelve or later) in various gambling houses, and all I could make him promise me, after he several times had become very indignant when I took the liberty to admonish him, was that as soon as he had won back the 200 piasters he had lost, he would only play at one house that was open only in the evening! He had arrived in Mexico a few days before I did and had already made enough progress during a two-week period that I must assume that before the end of May he either had hanged himself or worked for the hangman for a later opportunity.

I have mentioned the famous Spanish dance *fandango* and can thus here mention the Mexican amusements I have witnessed. The lower classes cannot live without their fandango and, as I have already mentioned, every Saturday evening or, rather, night there are dances at a public square. I watched it several times in Tampico. In Mexico City, that was not advisable for a stranger, and even in Tampico the evening's amusement seldom ended without fights and murder. The fandango is the most monotonous dance one can imagine, with 5-6 couples facing each other in the center of the circle. With guitar and violin music and a no less monotonous nasal singing, they shuffle to each other and, from time to time, change positions, then a man shuffles alone and a woman alone, and that is the entire famous fandango. I have been told that it is often accompanied with indecent gestures, which is possible, but the ones I saw were as decent as one could wish. Another national dance, *el bolero*, is more complicated and the music more beautiful, although the singing is always through the nose. Several other dances are also originally Spanish, but are only performed in the theaters. At the more elegant balls, they dance a Spanish Quadrille full of very beautiful and complicated figures, and waltzes, where the cavalier continually cuts capers around his lady and they both continually change the positions of their arms. This has too little grace to be considered beautiful.

Before the expulsion of the Spaniards, there was an Italian opera here managed by Garcia, who was very well-known in the United States and France, and it is said to have been very well attended. The shows are now as bad as the building is in disrepair. The orchestra is not bad, and the ballet exceeded my expectations in both the beautiful costumes and dance, and one could see that this was the favorite art of the nation. The exterior of the building does not compare to the rest of the large buildings in town. It is less than mediocre, and the halls are dirty and so low that I had to stoop to walk through to my seat. The interior still shows remnants of its former splendor in the various decorations, but the tooth of time has gnawed all over, and so little is being done to stop the destruction that, rather than replacing the broken glass in chandeliers, they have been completely removed and thus have reduced the already poor lighting and at the same time filled the house with smoke. When one adds the cloud of tobacco smoke from the audience, both women and men, with the exception of a few women in the balcony whom I did not see smoking, one can imagine the status of lighting in the hall. It was very big, especially in depth, and could probably seat 5-6,000 people. On the days where there are ballets, only about a tenth of that number shows up. There is bigger attendance at the *los toros*, or bullfights, which take place twice every Sunday. Although I knew that they were cruel, I could not resist my curiosity to watch a show about which I had read and heard so much without forming a clear picture of its nature. I will try to tell it in a way [so] that my readers will not be able to say the same.

Imagine a circle of two-story loges an average of 100 to 200 square feet each, built of wood — a very nice circus with stone walls fired years ago, and they cannot afford to build a similar one today — open in the center, so that one pays two prices, one for the shady side and another for the sunny side. Within the loges is a walkway, almost six feet wide, whose wall is massive wood five to six feet tall and which serves as an escape for those who torment the bull when they are pursued, and since it often happens that the enemy jumps over the fence, this is provided with gates, which close off the hall at the same time that they open the way to the arena so that the bull is right back in there. Before the start of the battle, the place is full of vendors of oranges and sweet lemons, selling them to the people in the loges, adroitly throwing them to the buyers, who throw down their money. The music started and a pair of decorated mules entered through a gate splinter-bar, which was used to drag out the dead bull. They were led around the arena a couple of times by a driver dressed in an old Spanish costume, and then made room for the other actors in this bloody game. Everyone was dressed in old-fashioned Spanish dress. They consisted of two *picadors* on horseback, or rather on jades, since they choose not to sacrifice the best horses to the horns of the bull, six or eight men on foot with colored banners, and finally the *matador*, or killer, in a red suit and with a rapier at his side. After greeting the audience, the riders placed themselves on either side of a gate in the fence, armed themselves with lances, the gate was opened at the blast of a trumpet, and a wonderful bull with fiery eyes came in. Without looking around, it immediately attacked one of the riders, who kept it back by pushing his sharp lance in its back by leaning in with all his strength. The horse yielded more than the bull, which, when unable to get close enough with its horn, turned on the other rider, who took the same advantage as the first one, but his poor horse stumbled at the violent push and the bull went over it and after him. In a moment, he was back on his feet and across the fence, but the angry animal was so close that one shuddered at the sight of it.

Under the cries of "*olé*" from the audience, it now turned on the picadors, who were on foot and starting to irritate it with their banners, which it pursued while they escaped by jumping aside and adroitly placing their barbs on its forehead. The barbs had small sticks with multicolored ribbons attached that dangled before its eyes and made it absolutely furious, but that was not enough. They now brought in fireworks, which they fastened to the head of the animal, putting themselves into a terrible peril. The fire and the noise of this brought the animal to the highest degree of madness, and if the pursuers had been less quick in their movements, it could have cost many people their lives, although the tips had been sawed off of the horns. Now, a clown appeared with a white painted face, riding a donkey with its foal behind them. He was stopped right in front of us, and that was just as well because in just a moment, the bull had thrown him down, and he escaped only through the help of the others, who with their banners made it attack them. The matador now came out with a red flag in one hand and his drawn saber in the other. The art is to stab it right in its heart when it attacks the flag. This time, he was unfortunate enough that the bull pursued him after being stabbed, which resulted in the rabble piping him out and another having to take the saber. The poor bleeding animal, with foam around its mouth, finally collapsed and was stuck by a knife in the neck, thereby ending its life. The mule team now came and dragged it out.

This was repeated four times without anybody getting killed — with the last bull this often happens, since audience members with their capes are invited to take the place of the picadors and often too many come in at one time or they are not quick enough to evade the bull. Should one fall victim to this unnatural amusement, they give a shout of *"olé"* for the bull, but nary a sigh for the unfortunate man. An ennobling pastime, completely worthy of a race of slaves, whether it crawls beneath the scourge of despots or that of a corrupt clergy.

The Spaniards and their Mexican descendants are great admirers of beautiful walking paths, and in Mexico City, there are two impressive ones. One is called the Alameda and is used very much during the winter until Easter. The other one is located farther away along a very beautiful canal that connects the city to a lake to the south from which almost all foodstuffs are delivered, and it is used mainly from Easter till Pentecost and is simply called *el Paseo* [the walking path]. Alameda is a square with a fence around, which is closed at night. Farthest out, along the wall, is a road for coaches and riders, and inside, are regular paths with stone benches and a fountain in the center and surrounded by several mediocre sandstone monuments. Only people of the lower class come to the inner part, while the better classes keep to the road, and between it and the wall is a row of tall elm trees and a walking path. But you must not for a moment believe that a lady would set foot on the so-called walking paths, they are only for the men! All the ladies stay in their coaches and ride around in a long row or sit still watching those who drive past. The coaches themselves are very ugly; the box is nice enough, but the undercarriage is *à la Fru Kløcker*, but lacking a coachman's seat. Instead of being a long cart with one iron rod in the center, it is made with two long wooden poles, one on each side and very massive. In order to be able to fit under this, the front wheels are very small, especially in comparison with the gigantic rear wheels, which follow a half mile behind as if they did not belong to the cart. The wheels are just as massive as the long cart, and on the more elegant ones, they are painted green with rich gilding. The coachman rides on the near wheel, and there are never more than two donkeys pulling the carts, no matter how heavy they are. It does not look very good, no matter how fancy the harness may be. All one can see of the city's beauties, and there are many of them here, is through the relatively small windows of the coach. It is hard to believe that nobody has considered importing *landaus* or *barouches* in this beautiful climate, where the ladies never walk except in the mornings when they go to mass.

On one Sunday afternoon, there were without a doubt 500 coaches on *el Paseo*, among them was only one open one and it belonged to the English minister. The most beautiful women in no ordinary toilettes peeked through every window, but it was, unfortunately, impossible to guess anything about their shape, footwear or bustles. Many gentlemen were riding their horses, and that is the way they kept moving in long rows back and forth on the long pathway, or stopped along the sides of the road for several hours. Meanwhile, the canal resounded with the singing and playing of guitars by members of the lower class, who had been amusing themselves down by the lake and were now returning on big flat-boats. Everyone, both men and women, was tidily attired and decorated with ribbons in all sorts of colors, while singing and playing and with cigars in mouth, they danced their fandango in the center of the boat. This was a pretty sight, especially since the opposite side of the canal was full of well-cultivated gardens and summer-houses and farther down, green meadows and the so-called floating gardens or small islands, which were formed by branches of the canal and in which vegetables were growing.

I just mentioned that the ladies only walked to mass or in the morning, and that is literally true, with the exception of late evenings, when they would stroll with their cavaliers up and down the archways (which looked exactly like the ones around the castle square in Copenhagen) and sit on the steps of the shops, a strange choice, which is mainly followed when there is a ball at the Foreigner's Club. This is located nearby and only God knows the reason why it is not protected by the leading Mexican families. One would expect that after the taste and splendor with which their balls are characterized, and the natural desire to dance that rules all classes. It shall remain unsaid whether it is because no local gentleman is admitted unless he is a member of the club, which is very expensive, especially because the English are its leaders, or because neither men nor women are allowed to smoke in the dance hall, although there is a smoking salon next door for the fair sex. But it is certain that none of this removes the natural curiosity of their gender from the ladies who do not participate, and so to satisfy it, they stroll through the archways and sit on the thresholds, where they can observe everyone coming and going. When I first arrived, I assumed that there had been a contagious illness since all the ladies I met in the street were wearing black. This, however, is the fashion; or rather, an ancient custom to which every woman of the better classes must submit if she wishes to avoid being ridiculed by the street urchins. They cannot let themselves be seen in the morning without being dressed in black silk dresses, black scarf and a veil on their heads. Only in the afternoon can they wear various colors. The men do not, of course, follow any rules, and the beautiful Mexican costume was only worn by the lower classes, especially in rural areas. It can be very magnificent and cost up to 700 piasters, and consists — to begin with the most important part — of a pair of green or violet velvet trousers, open on the outside from the knee down, and with both outside seams richly ornamented with round silver or plated buttons. On both sides and the front is silver or gold embroidering, and in the opening from the knee down the lower part of white and wide underpants is visible, stretching down to the ankle. The foot is covered with a shoe of the old Spanish style, the inside much higher than the outside, with iron spurs artistically made and exactly like the old knights' spurs. They do not use suspenders, but the trousers, which go only to just above the hips, are held up with a sash of red or green silk with rich gold fringes on both ends. The upper body is covered with a very short chintz blouse, which in most cases hangs over the left shoulder, and on their head, they wear a black or gray broad-brimmed hat edged with a gold braid, and around the crown is wound braids of gold, silver or pearls.

Since this is a nation of riders, the costume would not be complete without a beautiful horse with Mexican saddle and halter, gold and silver embroidered, and with covered stirrups in the old Spanish style. Their leather embroidery here is very artistic and tastefully done. In order for the rider, or rather the Mexican, to be complete, he must also have a cloak, a good quality of which is made in this country. They come in various colors, square, and with a hole in the center for the head. Together with this, which covers the upper body, plus a pair of *armas de pela*, or bearskins that hang together in the middle and are adapted to cover the legs, and the lower part of which is covered with *botas*, or a piece of hide, which they wind around the calf so that it covers the shoe, the Mexican rider can face the heaviest shower without getting soaked through. The cloak is an indispensable piece of clothing to the Mexicans, and even in the hottest sun they have it on or around their shoulders. Most people here in Mexico wear clothing like that in Europe, and it is unbearable to see them wrapped up to their noses in these cloaks when the temperature is 80° Fahrenheit, where we in Europe would appreciate the summer with... [sic], and if a north wind comes up even outdoor workers will leave their tasks to seek shelter or wrap up in their cloaks, and at the most keep one eye visible.

After having mentioned the rider, I should not forget his horse. It is a small breed, but very fiery, and a large horse *de paso* brings a high price. The *de paso* means a quick step, which they are taught and which takes away all aggressiveness from the horse, although it can keep up with the strongest trotter. In order to make the horse perfect, it needs to carry its head high and continually lift its front legs high, its age is then not taken into account, and I have often wondered whether the buyer would even check to see if the legs were flawless. The paso pace is obtained by riding them from the very beginning with a round leather cover over the hind quarters, the lower part of which reaches almost to the middle of the horse's thigh and is edged with a heavy iron bow on which many small iron rings of various shapes are fastened and rattle when the animal moves. This weight on the rear end provides the steady pace while at the same time it damages the hind legs, which on all of them bow inward so that when the horse stands, the knees are touching each other. This is also done to the mules that are meant for riding.

No foreigner should leave Mexico without having visited the fruit market. It is at a large, regular square south of the palace and is a veritable labyrinth of booths made of reeds and thatched with leaves; these are filled with baskets containing the most beautiful fruits in a volume and variety that one has never seen, unless one is familiar with this latitude. It is a striking sight. The European fruit found among them, such as pears, apricots and some variety of cherries, are only mediocre, and I do not believe that the great heat and long dry season of this climate are suitable for our fruit trees, which the geography books also tell us. The native fruits, on the other hand, were excellent, although only a few were to my taste. Several gave off a pleasant aroma, especially the pineapples, which were piled high. Many people, especially women in their blue striped head scarves, squeezed through the narrow aisles, which echoed with the vendors' offers and presented a very lively show. Many half-naked boys with baskets ran among the potential buyers to offer their services as carriers, and probably also to steal something if the opportunity arose. In this description, we must again remind you of the colors of the many faces, most were yellow; many were white, brown, and some black.

Close by and behind the castle is the old botanical garden. It is not as big as "Kultorvet," but it is a true picture of the Mexican republic, full of the rarest trees and plants. But the weeds are almost as tall as the trees, and it is in such a poor shape that one has to know one's plants in order to distinguish the good ones from the bad. But here, as in the Republic overall, there is the need of a capable and strong hand to get rid of the harmful growth and conserve the good, which with better care would bloom and flourish.

The weeds and neglect have not as yet been able to eradicate a few very remarkable trees; this is the so-called *flor de la manita*, or the "hand flower," in the exact shape of a hand and a beautiful red color, and it is found only two places in the world, namely, here and somewhere else in the Mexican republic. It has not been possible to transplant it into a different soil. The tallest tree is about sixty-eight to seventy feet tall and covered with flowers all year round. I took some and preserved them in alcohol and sent them to Professor Hornemann in Copenhagen. The old manager of this chaos bragged about all of his curios, and especially his merits in collecting and *sorting* them, as if he were Linnaeus himself, and he had the plants' genealogical tables hanging on his wall. Someone more easily provoked to laughter than I am would have difficulty getting away without getting into arguments with the man.

A new botanical garden has been established outside of town near the former viceroy's summer palace, and they say by a skilled man and on a very solid footing. I did not visit it since I am unknowledgeable and would hardly have enjoyed seeing plants that were yet undeveloped. It is not difficult to establish such a garden here since all plants grow out in the open, and all they need to thrive is shelter against the north wind and plenty of water. The afore-mentioned pleasure castle was built almost a century ago in a beautiful style on a high hill, which either by nature or artificially is plenty big for both the castle and its outbuildings. The garden is below and no matter how neglected it is, it still bears the characteristics of its former splendor. There is a beautiful view from the castle's terraces, and there is no doubt that this is the place from which the city looks the best. Here, on the west side, the area is better populated and the land is green, since even the lightest rain causes it to flood, and even now, when there has not been much rain, the cattle stand in water to their knees. One branch of the city's beautiful water line starts at a spring near the castle. It is built from rocks and brick in clay with a width of almost 12 feet and is 10 feet high, over which the water flows for about a mile in two branches. The difficulty in maintaining and repairing such a work, especially here, is all too obvious, and the water leaks through in many places in spite of much patching. This is another costly work done by the Spaniards which is now being neglected, although the sewers and the water mains under and from the city are very important to the city, and many thousands of Indians had been forced to build them. On one end, they had to blow a deep and wide diversion of several miles in the rocks and dig canals under the city in all directions.

Although I hear that the city government is not bad and that householders pay considerable taxes for public works, these canals are so clogged up in places that after every shower, which without exception came every afternoon I was here, accompanied by thunder and lightning as if the earth was going to perish, the streets get so flooded that it is possible to sail a boat from one end to the other without risk of getting stranded. One day, I was invited to dinner at the house of a French doctor who had been recommended to me. A couple of hours before I was to leave we had our predictable thunderstorm. The coach I had ordered did not come, so I started out on foot after the rain stopped. The first streets I passed through were rather high or their drains were open, so I got through without getting wet by staying close to the wall and now and then jumping from stone to stone. When I reached the street where I was going, there was a veritable lake in front of me, and although the doctor's house was just diagonally across from the corner where I stood, I seemed as far from it as I could be. Since it started pouring down again, I saw no other solution than to get onto the back of one of the rascals who competed in offering their services, when a cart came down the street and brought me across for a fair sum. It otherwise appears to be the custom to use these two-legged donkeys on such occasions, and Doctor Chabert told me that one time when he had done that and they were in the middle of the street, some fellow walked up and just took his hat from his head and walked away with it, although he yelled loudly to stop the thief. His yelling just drew more witnesses and bigger laughs.

During the three weeks I spent in Mexico City, my two servants had nothing to do except take care of the animals and enjoy themselves at my expense, and already on the first day, I got so tired of seeing them around that I asked them to spare me of their presence as much as possible. After this, I knew that when they came they needed money. I was not worried about my Portuguese and gave him almost as much as I knew I would owe him by our return to Tampico. The other one, however, could give me a good day when he wanted to, and then I could go chase my money. I was warned in that respect to be careful, since their conceited sense of honor is very tender, and if they felt that they had been wronged, they would always take revenge. Of this, I had a striking example in Tampico. On the recommendation of a merchant, I had hired a servant to accompany me on this trip, and we had agreed on the conditions. I had told him to look for some horses, and he came and told me that he had found one that would cost 30 piasters for him, but for a foreigner, it would cost 40. I asked him to get it and come and show it to me, and if I approved then I would pay the price. It is hard to believe that the Mexican sense of honor could be hurt by such a remark, but he canceled our agreement since he was unwilling to follow a master who had no faith in him. I later bought the same horse for 26 piasters! It was apparently his intent to cheat me. I now wanted to guard myself as much as possible against getting cheated and then later being an object of revenge, and offered to pay only part of what he asked for, but enough to assure that he did not leave me halfway through, and then I gave him some small trinkets to soften the blow. This good animal's way of life is noticeably an example of how few republican customs have yet made their appearance here, and how their entire upbringing is an imitation of Spanish and arch-monarchical customs. In the mornings when he came in, he always said: *"Buenos dias, Señor, cómo está Vm?"* [How are you?] *"Cómo ha pasado Vm la noche?"* [How was your night?] *"Cómo amanace Vm?"* (How was your morning?) Had I a wife and children, there would have been a question and answer for each one, and even complete strangers make those foolish compliments to each other before they state their actual errand. We never left a place before my Mexican had said: *"Buenos dias, Señores* or *Señoritas"* (even the most wretched beggars earn that title), *"Beso sus manor."* [sic; should be *manos,* transl. "I kiss your hands"], *"Vivan Vms Milaños* (May you live a thousand years!) *"Dios lo paga a Vm!"* (God grant you that!) and he would never leave before all of this had been related and answered.

At last, on May 6, I left this strange city, probably forever, for my return trip to Tampico and the United States. I had instructed my people to be ready at eight o'clock since I intended to send the Mexican ahead with a money train to Real del Monto, while I waited for the mail from Tampico, which would be here about noon, and I would then reach him at the first night's stop. I was very angry when they did not show up until 11 o'clock, and in my best Spanish, I let the Mexican know, since it was his fault. The Portuguese waited for me at the city gate, and he told me that the escort had also been late, so I did not worry about my clothes, which accompanied them.

A couple of good friends accompanied me part of the way, and we stopped in Guadalupe to see the strange cathedral, which I should not have postponed so long. When we reached the door, there was a long line of people waiting to get in, since this was "Foot-kissing of the Holy Virgin," and for such a great honor and ceremony only a few could be let in at a time. After having waited in vain for half an hour, we realized that if it was going to take as long as it had for the others, by the time it came to my turn, I would not be able to reach my night quarters before dark. We thus wisely left the church, although I regretted having postponed such an important visit to the last minute.

A quarter of a mile past Guadalupe, I took leave of my companions and again found myself on the road where the first time I had experienced so much unpleasantness, although no real danger. I did not know what was awaiting me. There were no actual robbers to worry about except between Mexico City and Real del Monte, and the English escort, which I intended to follow, left me nothing to worry about in that respect, and there was no thought of other traveling companions. The day before my arrival in Mexico City, two foreigners had left the city for Tampico, but since then I had not been able to locate anyone who would be going there. They all advised me not to announce my wishes in the newspaper, since that would most likely attract the attention of robbers rather than of travelers. Fortunately, I had only had slight hopes of finding traveling companions, and was therefore as calm as when I arrived. There were no shortages of evil warnings, and I was yet to go through a trial different from the one on the trip here, but luckily, it was only short and bode as little evil as all of the other incidental occurrences which superstition and ignorance from ancient times have considered to be preventatives against subsequent real happenings.

My friends had hardly left me when I noticed black thunderclouds gathering over the mountains and the rain pouring down several places.

My hope that I would be able to avoid them by riding faster lasted only a short while when a whirlwind arose, and a moment later there was a downpour on our heads the like of something I had never before seen, even less had been under in an open field. My cloak, which I had wrapped around me, was not only soaked but was torn away from my legs in an instant, and it was not long before I did not have a dry thread of clothes from my thighs downward. The wind came straight in my face, and the horses, who would soon be in water to their knees, did not obey spurs or whip, but turned and stood with their backs to the wind. With difficulty, we finally got them moving again, and after almost a half hour of this soaking, we finally got under a roof, where we waited with many others for the rain to stop, which happened after another half hour.

We then waded on with water sometimes reaching the bellies of the horses before we reached an almost half-mile-long stone bridge leading across the plateau, which cannot be crossed during the rainy season. It is built of boulders and brick in clay and is an expensive project, and as with so many other things, it seemed odd surrounded by untilled fields with wretched sod shacks. The sharp stones with which the bridge was paved made it impossible to ride faster than a walk, and meanwhile our wet limbs were whipped by a cold, north wind, which at the height of the bridge seemed twice as bad, and I felt so cold that if I had not known that the sun recently had warmed my head I would have doubted that I had left the cold zone. Finally, the road changed direction at an inn at the end of the bridge, and it seemed less cold while the rain continued. The road was higher and dry, so that we were able to ride faster, and by sunset, we reached Ozamtilla, where the English escort was spending the night. For that purpose, the English company had erected a building with an archway, the courtyard of which could be closed, and there were many rooms for all the armed men who accompanied the wagon with the money.

I first inquired about my man, since I wondered why he did not stand at the gate waiting for me, and I was very surprised when they told me that he had left them halfway here after talking for some time with an old fellow just where the road goes up into the mountains, which are full of robbers. They did not doubt for a minute that he had taken off with my clothes and they advised me to go after him before it got too dark, if the value of it was worth the risk. Besides my clothes, the mule was also carrying my travel money in my trunk. No matter how great my loss, I was only one day away from Mexico City, where I could get everything I needed for my trip. I decided that this loss was not big enough for me to risk my life, since there were two possibilities: either he was a rogue, in which case I could only retrieve my property by force. Even if I was lucky enough to locate it, which was doubtful, and he would hardly be alone; or, he was an honest fellow, in which case he would show up without my having to tire my horses again, and, wet as I was, risk myself and my health. For that reason, I did not want to send my Portuguese either.

Meanwhile, it got to be eight o'clock, and then nine, and still the rascal did not show up. I started making preparations to return to Mexico City and to the loss of 4,500 piasters, since although I had no proof of his dishonesty, he was a Mexican and might be avenging himself for having been called those well-deserved names this morning. He might also be afraid of facing me, since I had understood from the Portuguese that the reason he was late was that he had sold one of the horses that we had agreed should go with us to serve in an emergency. It had been needed on the way here, and I had fed it the entire time in Mexico City; and just the day before he sold it I had had it re-shod (not unimportant here). Besides this, he had received higher wages than he deserved, and what he had bought with this was also on the mule as well as the Portuguese's grocery chest.

On the other hand, the rain could have forced him to seek shelter in the inn at the end of the stone bridge, or they might possibly have seen him and what direction he had taken. I therefore asked the innkeeper here if he would send a trusted man with a note to his colleague and ask him to tell my fool, if he were there, to get started so he would be here at the inn before the escort left at 5:30 o'clock the next morning. The man wrote a note and sent a young man, whom he had instructed not to tell anyone about his errand and without delay to bring back a response. The area was so unsafe that he was not even given permission to visit his relatives in the village out of fear that they would get the impression that the missing mule carried a valuable load and then rob it when it arrived.

I now had to go to rest, although the possibility that I would enjoy it had never been worse for me. My room lacked only a little in being as well furnished as the others we had seen on the way; that is, there was neither table nor bench — nothing. I cannot [say that] the walls were as bare as the floor, because in one place [there was] a stick with a hole, which served as a candle holder as well as any other piece of furniture a good imagination could create. Mine was poor enough that it was unable to conjure up a comfortable bed when I had to stretch out on a hard straw mat on the hard floor wearing my wet clothes and with my saddle as a pillow and the ceiling as a duvet, uneasy about the fate of my clothes and animals and angry at the thought that my good bed was now perhaps the resting place for the lazy body of some Mexican, while I had the pleasure of mortifying my flesh on a stone floor. Nonetheless, I was sleeping when the English guard at the gate came in with a light, followed by the young envoy who had returned from his mission and handed over his dispatches.

At first, I did not know from seeing the terrible scribbles whether the man, knowing the importance of the case and out of fear for his dispatches falling into the wrong hands, had used a diplomatic code language and forgotten to send me the key. But after having rubbed my eyes again and started with a, b-, a, ba- and so forth, I finally learned that my two animals had sought shelter from the rain and would be here early the next morning. They were already there when I rode past, and neither one (since the two-legged and the four-legged one were equally smart) had thought about keeping a watch on the road to stop us. More satisfied at the outcome than surprised by the stupidity of the animals, of which I had seen so many examples, I dismissed the courier and turned my other side toward the stones, hoping to find them a little softer than previously, and thus, I slept a little. My joy did not last long, however. Before long the Englishmen started stirring and getting ready and, before I knew of it, their heavy money-laden wagon rolled out the gate. My donkeys had not yet made an appearance, and it was 7:30 before they arrived, by which time my patience had again faced a hard test. All my clothing was soaked, and the Portuguese almost attacked the other man, who had protected his own so well that not a drop had hit it while his was dripping wet. There was no doubt about which one of the two was a loyal servant, and I could not keep from laughing at the thought of what a clear picture I once again had of "*la heróica Republica Mexicana.*" The English always travel hell-for-leather and kill many animals, and a beautiful horse collapsed when they arrived in the evening. When we arrived, we saw it where it had been dragged behind the building. The next morning, nothing but the skeleton was left, and I was assured that it had been eaten by wild animals. I was fortunate enough not to meet any of those poor eaters.

We were now alone on the road again; there was no question of overtaking the escort. To tell the truth, I was just as unconcerned without as with them. It had stopped raining, but it was constantly threatening, and my only worry was that this daily downpour in Mexico City and vicinity had stretched across the mountains and made the road impassable. I had been warned about this in Mexico City and advised to return through Vera Cruz or San Luis, but the first place is never healthy and I had no reason to risk my life by possibly having to wait two weeks for transportation. San Luis was just as far from Mexico City as Tampico, forming an almost right-angled triangle with San Luis in the center, or rather, in the straight angle so that it would take twice the time and cost double of what it would for this route. Besides, I would like to know whether the Indian to whom I had entrusted my lame horse had taken the opportunity to sell it or if I would find it and thereby its value again. I thus decided to take the same route back, and in the name of God, subject myself to whatever this decision would bring.

The English and the escort had told me that Mr. Tindall, the manager of the mines in Real del Monte, was on his way to Mexico City and that I would probably meet him. There are not many travelers and Europeans on this road and I should not need a further description. The only one I encountered toward evening I addressed as Mr. Tindall, and I was right. He invited me to go to his farm, where his wife and Mr. McIntosh would gladly welcome me. It was too late for me to reach Real del Monte before evening, but since I now knew the way, I planned it so that I would arrive the next morning in time to see the mines and then leave the following day, which was Sunday. I arrived at about 10 o'clock and was well received by the secretary, but it appeared that a guest was causing the lady some trouble, and it was 12 o'clock before I was dressed and able to meet her.

She was pretty, but cold and stiff, and I regretted that I had not gone to the town's terrible inn, especially since it was too late to go down in the mines.

There is no work on Saturday afternoon, so I would have to wait till Monday and thereby, lose two days if I was going to follow my original plan. In order to really see the mines, I would have to go down with the workers at 8 o'clock in the morning and come back up with them at four o'clock through a different opening, a distance of ½ mile underground. I would then have to go down about 400 *varas*, or almost 1,120 feet on long ladders that were wet and slimy, and then up again the same way. I must admit that no matter how interesting it would be to go through chasms which had contained millions and be eyewitness to the endless work which thousands of the most wretched humans must do to enrich just a few, my reluctance to lose two days, plus the memory of how tired I felt in Finland after just having gone 200 feet down, was enough to make me feel satisfied with what I could see above the ground and that was not insignificant. Besides that, for the one who is just curious, the various methods of working the different mines are not interesting enough that I personally, on an already exhausting trip, ought to take on more than the necessary difficulties that such offered.

When the revolution broke out in Mexico, the mines at Real del Monte belonged to, and had for centuries, the wealthy family of a Count de Reglas, which here had secured enormous fortunes. The troubles stopped the workers both here and in other parts of the country, and when the Spaniards were finally expelled from the republic, the mines were filled with water and the owners ruined. It did not take long before England's recognition of the new state got speculators and fortune seekers moving, and all of a sudden many mining companies were formed in London with thousands of pounds of capital, and they outran each other to become partners in the enterprises about which happy outcome there was so little doubt that the stock prices went 'way above their worth, and those who obtained them at the subscription price felt very fortunate. Engineers and agents were sent out to close contracts on old mines indiscriminately and naturally without regards to the price, which could never be too high for mountains of gold and silver.

The same principles were used in England. Workers were hired in high numbers and *"à tout prix,"* so that the domestic mines were almost forced to close due to lack of workers. Steam engines to pump the water from the mines were manufactured before they knew the condition of the mines where they were to be used, according to the wise principle that the man ought adjust to the dress, rather than the dress sewn to fit the man. Directors who knew neither the country nor the language were hired with princely equipment and salaries, and before the companies had received reports about anything other than the arrival of their agents, whole shiploads of all sorts of people and equipment left England. And before these landed in Vera Crux, the first fleet of gold and silver was already awaited in England. Never has such madness been carried out further or been better rewarded. Several ships arrived with their managers' ignorance and the participants' eagerness for this *brilliant* cause during the unhealthy season in Vera Crux, where half of them died. The rest of them had to seek inland and not only wait until the heat was gone, but until the roads became passable after the rainy season. They then had to send for their machinery, but the directors in London had expected roads and canals to be as they were in England. Since there was plenty of money and more was expected, the machinery was of the strongest, but also the heaviest kind and many of the parts weighed several hundred pounds. In a country where the roads are paths and the freight carts mules these machines came at a wonderful time, and it was first necessary to build decent roads before one could think of getting the machinery in, and it must have taken a long time before they could bring them up to the broken mines, where all the shafts were full of water. It thus, took a year before the machinery reached its destination, and several of them were returned to England to be replaced with different sorts after having tried at high cost and in all manners to fit them in. This did not cool the blood of the speculators, but the die had been cast and they had to face the facts.

As long as there was capital left, everything went well, but scarcely was it gone without the mines producing anything but water before the "gold harvest" people rebelled, and the consequence was that several companies folded if their share-holders did not want to throw good gold after bad following the initial losses. Many were in so deep that they did not feel that they could give up unless there were no prospects for improvement, and they kept on paying; among those good people were the owners of Real del Monte mines. It must truly be difficult to leave behind such an effort after having come so far that the weekly production is 10–12,000 piasters in silver, but expenses were at the same time 19–20,000, besides the tremendous cost of the establishments and interest on the capital. It has thus been a difficult hole to plug each week, and after six years, it has only been recently that the mines are producing. But hope keeps life going, and if they are lucky enough to have just one year of reasonable wealth, they might possibly, in a few months, recover all of their losses. This has been the case with another mine in Zacatecas, where they all of a sudden hit a rich vein at the same time that the order to cease work had already left London. The price of this company's stock all of a sudden rose above par.

Once bitten, twice shy, and after preposterous extravagance, order and thrift now reign. At least, here at Real del Monte, everything is arranged on an excellent footing. There are almost 100 Englishmen, among them are the first mechanics, who maintain the steam engines and make all of the various tools required on the job. Their shops are arranged as in England and equipped with all necessary tools, which, for a great part, are made locally. Their iron, copper and brass is all imported from England, although there are plenty of mines here, but the cost to mine it is too high. The Mexican government is so liberal towards the foreign mining companies that they can import everything they need, duty free.

The mines are worked day and night, and the steam pumps also work without stopping. The workers are relieved regularly, and I was there when they changed shifts. They have some sort of a hymn they sing the whole time, and there is something solemn in hearing the many voices disappearing deeper and deeper in the ground. They all have a broad hat to which is attached a lantern by which they can see to work. They do not just drill and blow up the hard rock wall, but also cut up the rocks and separate the pieces with silver ore from the rocks. The silver is put into small bags and the gravel in bags made of rawhide, and the gravel bags are winched up by horses, while the bags with ore are carried on their heads and backs out of the mines. They are all excellent judges of metals, and in order to encourage them not to choose the softest rocks to work through, but the richest, they get, in addition to their daily wages, 1/8 of the ore they cut out, and the manager has the authority to purchase it if he finds it acceptable. The mineworkers' income is supposedly not bad, but in our opinion, far from sufficient compensation for the dangers involved in their work, among those are the ladders that they continually must climb up and down in the dark. The blasting of the ore costs many limbs and lives no matter how experienced they are in separating the layers and drilling in the correct direction, and the drilling is the hardest work one can imagine. Mexican mining laws are excellent in almost all respects, and one of their sections states that silver gravel carried by the canal and silver ore that may still be in the previously sorted rocks, belong to the maimed and old mountain folk.

There are approximately 2,000 workers in the mines in Real del Monte, and one can imagine the kind of organization it takes to make sure the company was profitable. It was divided into different departments, each with a Mexican manager, and a certain number of these are under an English engineer. To prevent the ore from being stolen, each worker is searched when he comes up from the mine and again before he leaves the premises. In the inner part are workers who sort the ore and chop off even the smallest desirable parts from the rock. The silver ore is then packed in sacks and brought on donkeys to the smelter, which is about two miles away. The sorting is done by boys and young men and is a very slow process, since each little rock, often about the size of a fingertip, has to go through their hands, be inspected, and many times chopped off, but they are very quick and know what they are doing. All of these workers are paid on Saturday afternoon, and I enjoyed having a chance to observe this. It was done by four English policemen who sat by as many windows in a low building that divided the yard. Outside these windows, a couple hundred of these brown robber faces stood dressed in hide, receiving their and their absent comrades' wages. When a name was called, it was answered with "*Ave Maria puríssima*" or just "*Ave Maria*," and the number of workers or days' pay he was receiving such as "*A.M. p. cinco*" [five], "*A.M. cuatro*," etc. It sounded quite funny, and I remember that I had read in a travel description with my sisters that this was an unavoidable way of greeting in Spain, where the answer is: "*Sine piccuto Concibida*"] conceived without sin]. That is not the custom here, but my gallant Mexican probably would not have failed to add this greeting to his other long strings of words.

After having visited with Mr. McIntosh on horseback and the other workers connected with the mines and seen all the steam engines in operation (they had four by now), there was nothing else for me to see above ground. Several of the gentlemen invited me to accompany them to the smelting works, la Regla, on the following day, which in Tampico had been recommended to me as being an oddity. I must now add a few words about these mountain-dwellers. It is well-known all over that mountain folk are superstitious, and that in a country that is already very superstitious they must be even more so is natural. Everywhere one looks the mountains are embellished with crosses, and the English engineers themselves utilize these signs in their measurements, which adds much to their acceptance. They also have the same defects as their countrymen, and probably the tendency to quarrel to a higher degree, so it often happens that when they are called back to work, especially after a holiday, several are missing, having been stabbed to death in fights. Therefore, the company has found it necessary to call soldiers to Real del Monte to keep the workers in line. These heroes have very little to do most of the time (like in more civilized states where they are less numerous) and, probably more to kill time than to carry out their duties, they confiscate all weapons unless accompanied by a "*licencia de armas.*" This is required as well as a passport; but I arrived without a licencia and left without a passport. This causes more unreasonable difficulties than in Russia, since in order to travel from the coast to the capital, a foreigner, if he goes by the rules — and luckily enough this does not happen very often — must secure a government pass from his country's minister or consul in Mexico City. This can take at least six to eight weeks during which the traveler must amuse himself at the coast where he landed. Such an intolerable regulation is fortunately not followed very often, and I had a better reason to ignore it, since our country had neither a minister nor a consul in the republic, and the *alcalde* [Spanish: mayor] in Tampico stamped my passport from New Orleans, thereby assuring me that I would not have any difficulties. But nobody spoke to me about a *licencia de armas* [Spanish: gun license], and I have already mentioned that they stopped

From Rudolph's Diary:
His Gun Permit, Issued in Mexico

me in Guadalupe because of that, whereas nobody on the entire trip cared whether I had a passport.

Since I did not think that I would be that lucky on the return trip, I wanted to secure a passport in Mexico City and convinced myself that nothing could be easier. But, here too, a foreigner can only get one through his country's representative, and since Denmark, as I have mentioned, does not have one, probably in order not to offend the holy alliance, I went to the French consul general to inquire about the regulations. He advised me to go the ministry for foreign affairs. When I got there, they told me that I must first secure a passport from the governor of the State of Mexico; there they told me that I had to file a proper application in writing. I wrote up an application with a capital "S.S.G.S.M.B." or *su servido gue [que] sus manos beso* [your servant who kisses your hands], over my name as is done [*in a republic*] and went the following day for an answer. I was greatly consternated and regretful when I was told that my application had to be written on stamped paper and in a quite different style. I asked about the proper style, but the secretary (or whatever he was) was unable to help me and advised me to go to a notary, and after the application was found to be correct, I could return four to five days later and obtain my passport. All of this coming and going had taken up almost a week and I had decided to leave in two days' time. I thus bid the governor and the president a good day, got a *licencia de armas* from an *alcalde*, Don Ignacio José Montes dedea (whose signature took him at least 10 minutes to write and is so strange that I have kept the document as a curiosity), and started out without a passport. It was just as well, since nobody asked me about it; here in Real del Monte, however, they confiscated the weapons of my Mexican, and only by presenting my *licencia* did he get them back.

I hope one will forgive me this episode and pretend that it was the subject of conversation on the road to *la Regla*, where we headed on Sunday morning. We were Mr. McIntosh, the chief engineer, Mr. Tindall's brother, who is a physician, and myself. The main road down is very good; it is the same one I came up on my trip here through the derelict small town at the foot of the mountain, where the company had started smelting before they acquired the Regla, across a large plain where Anatoltonilco is located on the left, through a pine forest and past several farms that belong to the company for 100 years, along with vast stretches of fields and forests on the surrounding mountains. After riding for two hours, we finally reached a wide, paved road, which went rather steeply down around a cliff, at the foot of which we suddenly came to another gate, decorated with an old noble coat of arms and crosses, and it was not until it was opened that one was able to have a look at the many buildings of the works, among which was a church with a tower just inside the gate. It was quite an amazing surprise. It all lies as if in a hollow, surrounded by high mountains so close on all sides except the corner where the gate was, that even being inside it is hard to discern that it is possible that there could be room for all of the buildings and devices in the valley. There is such an abundance of water, even during the dry season, that the mountain stream is only in small part diverted to drive the many wheels used to pound and grind the ore.

All of this was established by the afore-mentioned Baron de Reglas family and from such sturdy materials that the English had to spend very little in order to get the works up and running. By virtue of their superior knowledge, they have been able to make considerable improvements that save much time and thereby expenses in the operations. Instead of using a large number of grinding apparatuses hewn from massive stone at a great cost and in terraces the way the Spaniards ground the ore, the English have built a large water wheel that powers a stamping mill which crushes the rocks in much less time, and this probably cost 1/500 of that of the grinding system. After the ore has been crushed into fine dust, it is put into piles and mixed with quicksilver, but this mixture must be perfect. This is accomplished by the dough, which looks like the most repugnant dirt, being trod by mules for several days. The influence of the air further expedites the amalgamation. It then goes into a funnel-shaped waterwheel where the dirt is rinsed away and the silver and quicksilver settle to the bottom. This then forms a compact mass which is then separated in the smelting furnace, where the quicksilver evaporates and is recaptured, and the silver is left and cast into the shape they wish to give it.

Two young Englishmen manage this, and they received me with great hospitality. I stayed for dinner and the night, and the next morning, I continued on my journey, which I hoped to continue straight to Tampico, and I was not disappointed. We crossed the enormous mountain canyon at

Rio Grande at a different and not nearly as bad location. I was glad that my macho was doing so well and had just mentioned this to my Portuguese, when just like last time, almost in sight of *St. Pedro de las Bacarillas*, it lay down several times and I feared more pranks. But we did reach my acquaintances in St. Pedro without losing much time, and I took my dinner there. The priest had gone and the church was locked. I was sure that I would be able to find a mule for sale here, and I wanted to buy one in order not to risk getting stranded on the road, being aware of the difficulties after my trip up. Fortunately for my wallet, the donkey drovers with the broken-in mules were away getting some corn and unable to sell me one. My macho got to Tampico with its load without further accidents. It was very comforting to me to see that the water level in the Rio Grande was low and the fields were as dry as when I came before, since nothing could be worse than water on this road, where the river had to be waded across numerous times and 3/5 of the distance is through low clay ground through thick forests where the sun cannot reach the forest floor. Since I knew the road and how far apart the houses were, I was able to arrange my daily trips much better. I thus took the liberty, much against my cavaliers' good advice and comfort, to cover eleven to twelve Spanish miles each day, which got me from St. Pedro to Tampico in six days instead of the ten it had taken on the way in.

We reached Cilacatipan around 3 o'clock in the afternoon on the 11th, and rested with our former suspicious host. I approached him, partly to ask about my shot-strap [perhaps a firearm accessory] and also to avoid his taking some kind of revenge on me out of jealousy from seeing me go to one of his neighbors. He had not seen the strap, but he had seen my shiny dollars and wanted make the acquaintance of their sisters. He thus tried to delay us in every manner, and my loyal servants were very accommodating in this. When he finally realized that I wished to continue, he used all his eloquence to talk me out of it, assuring me that I would be unable to reach a house before nightfall and before the threatening thunderstorm would hit. The latter was very likely, since it was very imminent, but I remembered seeing a house about a mile from here when we came up, and although it was getting late, I would rather risk the darkness and rain than stay with this rascal, whose guestroom (the chicken coop) was no more air- and watertight than God's open sky. And of two evils, it is better to get wet on one's horse than in one's bed.

My memory did not fail me, and just as the pitch-dark night fell over mountain, forest and valley, we reached the house, with corn and greens for the animals and food for my chaps. We were hardly inside before it poured down by the bucketful, and I thanked God for my good luck, since I had never seen a blacker darkness. In such a pouring rain, which made the mountain paths even more unsafe, to be by abysses where one misstep would be fatal would have been an extremely critical situation. The house was full of people and children, all of whom were busy scraping the grain [Turkish wheat and corn] from the heads and ears. A certain measure of this had already been sold to another traveler, and it had to be picked off or threshed, if you will, before they could go to bed. The children acted as candlesticks with lighted pine-sticks in their hands. With all of this going on, there was no thought about a place for my bed there, where, besides the emanations from so many, the heat was unbearable. I thus went to a small shed which served as grain storage and lay down on a pile of unhusked corn next to my already snoring Mexican.

We now faced the worst day of our entire trip, and one will recall that I did this part on foot on the way out. That was not my intention now, where the previous night's rain had made the road even worse, but a known enemy is not as bad as one that one has only heard mentioned as such. I now knew which part would be the worst and about when it would be over with, and did not hover between eternal fear and hope, which under such conditions is worse than even the most unpleasant certainty. I thus stayed on my horse, although it often threatened to get stuck in the holes in the clay, which were deeper than on the way up, and I only got off at the most steep rock slopes, where the horse continually had to jump or slide down on the sharp rocks. I was happy and content to reach Asonte a little after noon in a melting heat. My former hostess was sick and I went to her brother's to rest for a couple of hours. (He had ridden to the festival in Tampico el Alto, about which I shall tell more later.) We wanted to get to La Incada before evening, where I had left my lame horse. The Kanjade was still as dry as when we came up, and I was glad to hear that hardly any rain had fallen on this side of the mountains. My horse still stepped faint-heartedly across the rocks, but it now had four strong shoes and [so] I did not feel sorry for it. On its back, I thus passed 50 times across the Kanjade, and at dusk, I reached La Incada, which had been a little farther than I remembered. My first question was about my horse, and I was glad, not just because of the value of the animal, but also for the confirmation of the Indians' natural honesty, to learn that it not only was alive, but healthy and at my service. I was pleased to pay the man his two piasters and continue my trip at daybreak the next morning.

I had hoped to find pineapples in Asonte; there were none, but they had the tasty banana figs or plantains (as long as a hand and as thick as four or five fingers, soft and seedless). They were so cheap that I got 39 for one *medio* [ca. 12 skilling], while two or three cost one *real* (one rigsort [=1/4 of a 'rigsdaler' or Danish dollar—transl.]) in New Orleans. There was no other fruit in town at this time, but I saw that the oranges on all the trees between the houses in Asonte had grown much since my first visit and that with a little effort they could have plenty of all kinds of fruit all year. There was not a garden to be seen in the entire town. Although no rain had fallen since my trip out and all fields were scorched, the grass was green and there were the most beautiful flowers, among which a wonderful pink bell was especially noticeable. The birds were just as cheerful as before and just as pretty; as before, the small ones sang the sweetest sounds, while the parrots, the wild turkeys and some kind of raven joined in the symphony so that one had to cover one's ears. A true and clear picture of human society, where those who scream the loudest often have no assets other than a couple of stronger lungs.

After reaching Chicontepec in a scorching heat and resting there for a couple of hours, we arrived at a hacienda at nightfall and found hospitable people and everything we needed for ourselves and our animals. The heat was no less oppressive the next day, but the road was good, and we arrived in [Santa] Catarina by sunset. It was one of the most beautiful small towns one could imagine and (maybe with better neighbors) a philosopher could spend a happy lifetime here. I was again referred to the local prison to spend the night, and it seemed to me to be a good sign of the town's honesty, or perhaps only of the poor enforcement of its laws, that I was its only occupant. The children here, up to the age of 6–8 years, usually wear only a long shift, and the only possible addition was a flimsy petticoat. It appeared that nobody thought about taking exception to them, but when they see a stranger, they usually don't appear without a blue-striped bandanna on their heads that also covered their shoulders and chests.

An American doctor with whom my Portuguese is acquainted, supposedly very capable and with a large practice in the area, but unfortunately very hard of hearing, came and bored me for such a long time with his presence and questions that I finally excused myself and went to bed. I had placed my bed outside under the roof overhang where I could enjoy the cool night air, which had never felt better, and on the entire trip, I did not have a more refreshing and sweet slumber. My alert adjutants were of the same opinion, and the sun was high above the horizon before we departed. The consequence was that the most killing heat overcame us an hour after our leave-taking and pursued us the entire day through a palm forest (which does not provide any shadow against vertical rays of the [sun]), but does block the least breeze that might be in the air) with so much strength that a dog, which had followed us from Mexico City, was unable to tolerate the burning rays and stayed behind under a tree. We still reached Zurluama before evening and lodged in the prison, or rather, outside under an overhanging roof, where the guards, consisting of a couple of poorly armed citizens, were staying. They were only there at night, for what reason I do not know, since there were no prisoners, and they even asked us if we would not care to go inside where there were tables and benches and several lazy chaps stretched out themselves.

I thanked them for the honor, although a moment later I almost regretted not having secured a guard to shield me, not from robbers or wild animals, but — this sounds a little peculiar — from the colossal friendliness of a new American doctor, whom my [obliging] Portuguese again had jammed down my throat. After having assaulted me with questions à la Andreas H. and, among other believable news, telling me that a courier had just arrived from Tampico with a report that a fleet carrying 25,000 Spanish troops had been seen along the coast, he was offended when I expressed doubt about it and that they had attacked an American schooner which had come to Tampico to rearm. He assured me that he would do anything for one who *spoke English* and to prove it, he asked me to lodge in his house for the night; he would have a couple of bottles of wine brought in, and we could have a jolly evening.

I assured him that I was satisfied where I was and that I had no desire to drag all of my things to the other end of town. There was no help for it; I had to go and see his house. An immense stench of apothecary herbs met me when he opened the door; one of his two rooms lay filled with sarsaparilla, which he told me he had gotten *very* favorably (everyone else had lost money on it for several years). In the other was a table with several apothecary bottles and glasses, a chair, and a bed placed diagonally from one corner to the other in order to make room. I asked him where he was going to place my bed. "Oh, he would take care of that — maybe in the attic." He now told me that he was expecting his wife in a couple of days with his furniture, and then this house would become a true [but hardly sweet-smelling] heaven. I was careful not to doubt for a moment, but nonetheless asked him to excuse me if I did not show much desire to have a foretaste of it, and thus, I preferred to stay where I was.

I could hardly keep from laughing straight into his face when he seriously assured me that he could not understand what kind of man I was since I would refuse such an offer, which he swore that he did not make to just anyone. I could at least promise to come and talk to him for a couple of hours before he went to bed, since he could not tell me how much he had enjoyed talking with me. I now thought that the man was half-crazy and hurried home and to bed, but within a quarter of an hour, he came to fetch me. Wine was on the table and entertainment was ready; but when he found me in bed, he had to seek refuge with my Portuguese, who was easier to talk into going. He returned about ten p.m. and told me that the doctor would show up in the morning in time to see us off. However, in his stead came a hired man, demanding payment for the wine. The doctor, who had neither credit nor money, had put the wine on my bill, and here I found the key to his friendship. My Portuguese laughed heartily and advised the fellow to be more careful the next time. That was his payment, and the last I heard of my new friend were the expletives of his creditor.

A long and melting day's journey brought us to La Tortuga, where, on the way out, I had spent my first night and found the half-naked nymph kneeling behind the corn-grindstone. The strips of meat had been consumed a long time ago, and since they probably had to mortify themselves after such an unusual treat, my cavaliers were unable to even find tortillas there.

Finally, our last day of travel arrived and, with it, the end of all the uneasiness, worries and difficulties which accompanied it. Not since the beginning of Christmas vacations in my boyhood, and later, the days when I was reunited with my loved ones after an absence of several years, have I greeted a day with greater satisfaction. It was as if the heavenly kingdom lay open to me in the miserable Tampico el Alto, where, in a couple of days, the aforementioned festival was to be observed. It was proclaimed in everything, almost all of the houses had been whitewashed or in the process of being done. The church and the walls surrounding the cemetery were decorated with foliage, and everyone was as busy as if they were to celebrate a wedding in their own family. Never was superstition more clearly evident than on this occasion, where people come from many miles around to follow the procession to honor a saint who will appear on a ship in the air before true believers. All along both sides of the road to the village, vendors were already set up with the local fermented alcoholic drink *pulque*, and pineapples and cakes for the ones passing by, and the young people looked as happy as they do at home on a market day. The worst part is that it is for the benefit of ignorance and superstition!

I reached Tampico [de Tamaulipas] around noon, and to me it was as if I were home. Every face I saw seemed to be a childhood friend whom I was glad to see, as if we had been separated for years. But nothing seemed more wonderful than the meals, which, before my departure to Mexico City I had considered mediocre, and which since seemed to have gotten worse rather than better. I was satisfied, and the feeling of contentment I enjoyed after the difficulties I had been through and a most satisfactory conclusion of my business had a positive influence on my well-being. I was satisfied with the world and myself. My necessary stay in Tampico before departing for New Orleans was far from free from unpleasantness. I had difficulty selling my animals without a considerable loss, but what annoyed me the most was that a French merchant who had guaranteed me a price for the horse and mule I had purchased from him now preferred to break his promise to suffer a loss of 10 piasters. But the climate in which he lives had already influenced his strong moral character to a point that it was not considered shameful to be of *mauvaise foi* [insincere; dishonest].

The ship on which I was to make my return trip was waiting for the arrival of a *conducta* with piasters and silver bars from the interior. This is the country's leading export article, and it is not easy to find a better one. These escorts usually come twice a month, bringing on pack donkeys anywhere from 800,000 to a million piasters! The greatest share is exported to England on the mining companies' account, and much goes to the United States in payment for imported manufactured merchandise. A detachment of Mexican troops escorts them, and it is very seldom that they are attacked on the way, although there is often a civil war going on where they pass through. An English corvette calls at Tampico once a month and always carries away enormous sums.

On May 26, I finally left Tampico and *"la república Mexico,"* probably forever, but I took with me the memories of my experiences, and those will be dearer to me than the many piasters aboard the schooner *Hunter*, Capt. Refrito from Tampico to New Orleans. The most wonderful weather one can imagine favored our trip and the crossing took only five days. The Gulf of Mexico, which can occasionally be the worst waters on earth, had put on its mildest face without a single moment, as so often happens this time of the year, offering a wrinkle-free mirror, which not only bears witness to a perfectly calm sea, but also by its reflection enhancing the sun's hot rays. I thus did not spend a moment in my cabin from the time I got aboard until we landed in New Orleans, and that was just as well, because the day following our departure, it became a death chamber.

Our skipper, although one could see that he had a bad case of dropsy, came aboard and spent the first day on deck without any complaints. The following day the first officer told my traveling companion and me that he was suffering terribly, and we heard him groan off and on, but I did not think that his life was threatened until about five o'clock, when the first officer came and told us that the captain was dying. We had hardly gotten down there when he breathed his last. It was a strange feeling to unexpectedly witness a scene of death, which, fortunately for the deceased, as well as us, was of short duration, and so were the preparations for his *funeral at sea*. The new captain immediately had him brought on deck and sewn into the blanket in which he had died with some ballast in the end. I asked if the body should not be cold before it was thrown overboard, although it was very unlikely that it would come back to life, but I felt the simplest precautions ought not be ignored. All I accomplished by this was that a mirror was held in front of the mouth of the deceased, after which the body, probably not an hour after it had become such, was committed to its wet grave accompanied by the reading of a brief formula. All in all, this was not very solemn, and in such haste that I would have been suspicious of a lack of sentiment in anyone else other than this noble man, who now became the commander of the ship.

Return to New Orleans

Contrary to my expectations, I found the heat in New Orleans to be less intense than in Mexico City, but the air was more oppressive, and as a consequence, I suffered much more from perspiration. New Orleans has a low altitude surrounded by cypress forests which allow hardly a breeze to cool the hot air, while Tampico has a wonderful sea breeze and clean air. It was not long before I felt the effect of the heat on my constitution, and while it was far from alarming, it did cause a weakness which, combined with diarrhea I had brought with me from Mexico City, changed my otherwise healthy appearance and brought my acquaintances, especially of the fair sex, to encourage my rapid departure to the north. I did, however, not see the least danger in staying here, especially since I, by expeditious means, brought my rebellious subject back into line, and since new business had to be taken care of, it was my intent to leave New Orleans around the middle of July. Since I wished to make the forthcoming long journey with a friend who was unable to leave town until a week later, I postponed my trip until then and not until July 23 did we, *under full steam,* go up the King of Rivers, the proud Mississippi.

In the meantime, an event happened which I believe I ought to mention, since it casts a strong light on the youth of New Orleans and can save me a long thesis on local upbringing habits. A decent publican was walking home arm in arm with his wife one evening when a young man from a very fine family approached the wife, addressing some indecent words to her and making offensive gestures. The husband's remonstrances only made the fellow more daring, and thus, he found it necessary to resort to other means and gave him a slap in the face so that his hat flew off into the gutter and himself almost after it. He got up immediately, put his hat on his head, reached into his pocket and with a "Thank ye" put the barrel of a pistol against the stomach of the man and shot him. The man's screams and the sound of the weapon brought people running and the murderer was arrested, whereupon a large number of his friends and fellow topers did their best to free him. The following day his father posted a bond of 4,000 piasters, got him out and sent him away, although according to the law, if the man died, he should receive the death sentence. Such flagrant injustice caused a rebellion among the sailors who used to frequent the wounded man's pub, and they went to the jail to release all of the prisoners, who, they claimed had committed less serious offenses than the escapee, who was freed because he had money, while the others were poor. Fortunately for the police, they learned about their intention and armed the citizenry.

When the sailors came, they were easily overpowered; eighty of them were taken into custody, but were released the following day after a suitable reprimand. The consequences of this shameful action are inconsequential; it is the object itself I want to mention. It is too often an occurrence here that brawls over trifles among the youth are settled with sabers or pistols, but a killing such as the one described can only take place as a consequence of an extraordinary corruption; for this ample opportunity is provided by the many gambling and drinking establishments tolerated in the city, and which are extensively frequented by the youth of New Orleans. The lack of social intercourse among the families unfortunately also has this consequence - the worst that can be imagined. It is a shame that in a country like this justifiable punishment can be avoided by the payment of money. And should one reason alone — that the criminal carried around a loaded attack weapon – mean that he should go unpunished? Could 4,000 piasters, of which the victim does not receive anything, recompense such an offence, which is much the worse coming from a person who ought to know how disgraceful it is? One would not expect to see such legislation in America!

I left New Orleans in the company of about forty cabin and 100 deck passengers, and that same morning, I was told that the first outbreak of yellow fever had occurred the same day, so it was time to leave. The harbor was already almost deserted, and the usually so lively sight along the river bank now mostly resembled a cemetery, and the yellow dust clouds, which arose from time to time, yellow fever's foul spirits. One should be aware that at this time of the year almost all conversation is about health and illness, about the departure of acquaintances and fear for the fates of those, who despite advice from friends have decided to face the fever. One's thoughts thus center on this topic, and it leaves an unpleasant impression even on those who think and talk about death in a reasonable manner. Fear of the fever is what one must especially watch out for, since it alone can bring on the illness, and it takes much self-control to avoid becoming scared, when one hears all the talk about illness and death. It had not come this far by the time I left, and I had no reason to be afraid. Whether I would have avoided it later when the fever broke out in full force and attacked every unacclimatized foreigner is a question I naturally am unable to answer, and probably, as far as I am concerned, will never have an occasion to do so.

Heading North

The invention of steamboats was to the New Orleans trade what the art of printing was to the sciences; both underwent a total revolution, and luckily for the better. It has been 20 years since the first steamboat appeared on the Mississippi, and now there are perhaps 300 and up to 400 commercial ships' tonnage providing ample employment on its expansive length and the rivers included in its gigantic gulf. The name of the one on which I took passage was called *Huntsville* after its home city, many hundreds of miles up the Mississippi, Ohio and Tennessee rivers in the state of Alabama. The water at this time of the year is too shallow in the smaller rivers for the larger vessels to go there, and thus, passengers were only taken on the Huntsville to the mouth of the Ohio; from there are smaller steamboats, several with only an eighteen-inch draught, which are able to go to Louisville and Cincinnati any time of the year. From New Orleans to the mouth of the Ohio is almost 1000 English miles, and from there to Louisville, it is about 450, a stretch against a strong current which has been covered in nine days, but that was at a time when the river level was high, and the steamship was able to pass over places where it is absolutely dry during the summer. We had to follow the main channel, which involves the most unbelievable bends, and thus took much more time. Also, our boat did not have the most powerful engine, and we lost many hours due to maintenance. Another boat had left the city a day ahead of us full of passengers with the same destination. A few hours after our departure, we met it being towed back to New Orleans, since it already had a broken axle. Such, and even worse cases, if the boiler explodes, which unfortunately often happens on the river, with the loss of many lives, is not the only hazard on this route. The many tree trunks carried down the river often get caught by their roots in the river bottom, and their broken branches and the muddy water make those so-called snags invisible until they reappear on the surface. They have caused the loss of many ships by tearing holes in the bottoms.

Fortunately, very few think about the dangers involved in making such a trip, and we must again thank God that our future is swathed in darkness. For the first three or four days, there were sugar and cotton plantations along the riverbanks with small openings. Later on, the endless and uniform forests are seldom broken by other than the woodchoppers who had settled at the high points along the river to supply the steamboats with wood, which happened two times daily. Besides all the merchandise brought down on the steamboats, there was a larger quantity going to New Orleans on flatboats or barges that drift with the current and usually have a crew of three to four men, who constantly work with huge oars with which they steer the vessels. Before the invention of the steamboat, all merchandise was transported that way, and then the crew must walk the hundreds of miles back through wild and untilled land where there were no roads or paths. A round trip to New Orleans from Louisville took up to six months, frequently more than a year, and many difficulties had to be faced. Now, one can go by steamboat for only five piasters — when providing one's own food — and three if one will help load firewood during the trip! What a difference! It is thus no wonder that the population up north is increasing just as New Orleans is daily expanding its considerable mercantile industry.

All of the settlements along the river are located up high to avoid being flooded, since the river at times can rise 80 to 100 feet! I had difficulty imagining that since it was so low now, and this difference must also mean that the distance would vary when one is able to take shortcuts of many miles when the water is high. The river goes clear around the compass in its bends, and it continually erodes one side and drops it at the other. Sometimes it breaks clear through an entire tongue, whereby the distance is cut by 9/10 and more, and it is peculiar to see the regularity with which a new forest grows up on the river banks, as heavy as if it had been planted by man in levels according to age. The soil in Louisiana is very fertile almost all over, but up higher, it is less so; nonetheless, both banks are covered with impenetrable forests, and each settler must start with axe and fire before he can get any yield from the soil. The first city of any size we came to was Natchez, in the state of Mississippi; it was settled by the French before New Orleans was established. It was mainly populated by Indians whose tribe gave the city its name, but who were wholly wiped out by the Europeans and other wild tribes stirred up against them by the Europeans. Although it is located 300 English miles north of New Orleans and on high ground, it is as unhealthy during the summer as all of the towns in between. The heat was so oppressive when we arrived in Natchez that I did not want to climb the high river bank behind which the city is located. The ones who went ashore found it very attractive.

It was an entire week after we left Natchez before we saw another small town; this was Memphis, in the state of Tennessee, a hamlet surrounded by Indians who own plantations, Negroes and much livestock. The town is growing and is well established on a hill. Later on, we passed New Madrid, Spanish and one of the oldest settlements along the river. In 1812, the town was almost completely destroyed by an earthquake and many people perished. An island in the river by the town completely disappeared, and another one appeared a short distance from it. New Madrid is in the state of Missouri on the right-hand [sic] river bank and is insignificant. Since the river offered very little variety, many of the passengers on our steamboat naturally sought other means of passing the time, and there were plenty. From New Orleans on we had a professional gambler aboard who immediately opened his Faro-bank, and another one of the same ilk joined us in Natchez, who in the same manner, helped to lighten the load in our fellow travelers' pockets in the same noble manner. I do not believe the latter had much luck, or he would hardly have left on foot without paying when we reached the mouth of the Ohio River and run the risk of getting his limbs broken if our captain had gotten hold of him. Besides these noble games, there were several party games to which I remained an observer as I had of the others. There were plenty of books on board, and although the heat made it almost impossible to read, I preferred idleness over a pastime that could cost me money, and worse yet, regrets. The party was also made up of so many different people whose acquaintance I did not wish to make that [,so] the best thing for me to do was stay away from any kind of familiarity and other togetherness beyond the most necessary.

On the fourteenth day, after our departure from New Orleans, we arrived at the mouth of the Ohio River on the 37th degree latitude, a straight-line distance of seven degrees, or approximately 500 English miles, and along the river no less than double, or 1000 miles. Until now, the trip has been extremely monotonous. The changes started here and did not stop until we left the beautiful Ohio. Those rapidly growing states, Illinois, Indiana, and Ohio, have their southern, and Kentucky its northern border in this river, whose water is mirror clear, and whose banks offer the finest variety of forests, tilled fields, hills, high rocks, houses and villages. But it is mainly on the high or north bank that immigrants settle, since there is no slavery as in Kentucky, and while I recall seeing only a single new town on the south river bank, Henderson, there are many on the north bank, among them, Golconda, Evansville, Rome, Troy, Jeffersonville, New Albany, Madisonville, Bouville Vevay [a Swiss settlement from Canton de Vaud], all of which appear to be thriving.

The Ohio has many tributaries, almost all of which carry steamboat traffic almost six months of the year and all of which send their contribution of merchandise down to the markets of New Orleans: Kentucky, mainly tobacco and wheat flour; Indiana and Ohio, corn, flour and all kinds of provisions which from New Orleans are exported to the West Indies and South America. Both the Mississippi and the Ohio rivers are strewn with islands, but only the ones in the latter are partly inhabited and very picturesque, especially where the rocks rise high on both river banks broken only here and there by fields and gardens with plain but rustic buildings. In places, there are caves in the rocks, and one very deep grotto still bears the name "Robbers' Den" from the gang that used to attack and plunder the rafts on the river and, for a long time, got away with this without punishment, since there were no inhabitants in the area to bear witness against the robbers. It took months before the surviving relatives of those who were killed knew what had happened, without being able to find the place or the perpetrator in this wild country. But with increasing population and especially the introduction of steamboat transportation, this as well as many other evils disappeared, and there are no longer any examples of unsafe voyages from that source.

The first city of any size on the Ohio River, and it was for a long time the most important, was Louisville, established by the French in the middle of the previous century. It now has almost 12,000 inhabitants. It has had its share of the area's surprising growth and now has a considerable trade with central Kentucky, the state where it is located. Many steamboats continue to ply up and down the river from Louisville, and every day there are small steam packet boats going up to Cincinnati. The larger boats are unable to go that far at this time of the year, and many heavy ships stay at the shipping port [a ferry crossing] below Louisville for the summer. This is a distance of two English miles, and any merchandise going to or coming from the West must be transported over land. In order to resolve this difficulty, they were in the process of blasting a canal through solid rock, and this should be opened for shipping by the end of the year. During the dry season, both steam and barge traffic will then be able to pass through this most dangerous section and not have to wait for high water so that sometimes ice arrives and delays their return down river for several months, resulting in considerable losses.

We arrived in Louisville after four days in a beautiful and comfortable steamboat where the food was no worse than aboard the Huntsville. I spent some of the most wonderful moonlit nights you can imagine on deck watching the most beautiful scenery and felt no less satisfied than my fellow travelers who did their best to pluck the dollars from each other's pockets and to whom the jack of clubs and his pals was the loveliest phenomenon of nature and art. Although this was the slow season, we met many steamboats, some of which were stranded, and the water was no more than three feet deep in many places. There were many turtles swimming around with their heads above water; those are the first I have seen in the wild; but they are not very big and pulled their heads under the water when we got close.

We spent a day in Louisville in this terrible heat and visited New Albany [Indiana], a village across the river where my traveling companion had some relatives. This little town with a population of 2,300 saw its first house built in 1812 and will continue to grow at the same rate as the population of Indiana; it is one of the states where most immigrants settle. American villages are not like the European; large buildings with stone foundations and slate roofs are built right away, and one never sees any thatched roofs anywhere. On the other hand, they lack what makes our villages so rustic and picturesque—gardens, which Americans in general do not much appreciate. High wages are probably the main reason for that, and the settlers have many other more important things to do than gardening. I did not care much for Louisville, perhaps because I was fairly bored there and did not find the inn we put up at to be up to my expectations based on what I had heard about the inns up north. And I had expected reasonable prices, but everything was as shamelessly expensive as in New Orleans. Nor could I stand the unbecoming way the Americans swallowed their meals. I hardly finished my soup before half of the basins were empty, and the people who had sat down with me were already finished with their meal and running out with their mouths full. This unreasonable rush, just as unhealthy as it is indecent, is more habit than necessity, and that is probably the cause of the terrible illness that so many people suffer from and die of in America, dyspepsia, which I have never heard mentioned in any other country. They also ruin their stomachs by drinking grog and snacking all day long. One could recommend in vain a different way of living; it has already become second nature to them. At the table, they do not open their mouths except for a fork, and if they are at a party where they have to sit at the table for a longer period of time, they have another, perhaps even worse habit, namely, sitting and drinking port wine or Madeira for hours after the meal.

The farther up the Ohio River you get the nicer are its banks, and the short stretch from Louisville to Cincinnati is the prettiest one can imagine. We covered it in twenty-four hours, and I wish that I could have sat on the deck the entire time and enjoyed the pretty sight. We saw many Louisville steamboats; all had cabins on the deck and were very low in the water and of a pretty design and well maintained. On the entire stretch from New Orleans to Cincinnati [1500 English miles, 330 Danish], I did not see a single sailboat, not to mention pleasure craft. The Americans are too busy for that, and even in the big straits along the east coast, there are relatively few, especially compared to England. I thought that on the Ohio, where the current is not too strong, they would be able to use sails for the transportation of goods.

We arrived in Cincinnati [on] Aug. 6. I do not remember a city where my first impression had been this pleasant. A picturesque location on a high hill at a bend in the river, and new, massive three- and four-story stone buildings, forest in the background around the town and across the river, which is not very wide here, and on two lower hills the most beautiful villages with several sizable factories, a stream and fields and forests farther back. This is Cincinnati, a city the rate of growth of which probably is not seen anywhere else, even in America. It got its name from an association formed by returning officers after the Revolutionary War as a memorial to their suffering and brotherhood. The great Washington was their president, and they adopted the name of Cincinnati after the well-known Roman commander who left his plow to save his native land, and then returned when his service was no longer needed. A member of the Cincinnati Society also had a black badge, which they wore until envy was awakened among their fellow citizens, who did not feel that a true Republican should wear such a badge of honor for having done his duty to his native land. The badge and diploma are now passed on from father to son, and the former is worn only on special occasions, while the diploma is displayed in a frame on the wall. In 1808, this city was a wretched hamlet, as was the state of Ohio in which it is located. There was only an endless forest which, with the exception of a couple of forts built by the United States as protection against the Indians, was inhabited by wild men and animals. Cincinnati now has no fewer than 25,000 Indians, and the state of Ohio almost a million!

Life in Cincinnati seemed very pleasant to me and brought to mind the market days I have experienced in Danish towns. The town square was filled with wagons, all with four beautiful and fat horses and covered with canvas. They brought to town all kinds of provisions and fruits from the rich vicinity, and both the wagons and their drivers bore witness to a prosperity that always leaves a good impression with one's customers. The only thing that seemed strange to a foreigner, who is used to European peasant dress, is to see everyone dressed as gentlefolk, and while a shabby dress might be of more worth than a homespun coat, I would much rather see the latter on a farm wagon and behind a plow. But here in America, which has people from so many different countries, one cannot expect to see a national costume, and the political equality between the lowest and highest classes does not allow a peasant class as with us, which testifies to dependence and serfdom. This is especially noticeable among the women; in the middle of the most impenetrable forests, in a house built from rough logs, one may see women wearing puff sleeves according to the latest Paris fashions, silk ribbons with buckles around their waists and *coiffure à la grecque*. They all often have poor quality but clean neck wear, and in the bearing of many, one can clearly detect previous wealth and worldliness. A biography of the inhabitants of the American forests would offer more than one educational and entertaining aspect.

I am getting ahead of my trip through the state of Ohio — one episode I was present at and which is extremely characteristic brings me back to Cincinnati. There are several routes from here to New York. When the water level is high, the steamboats often go to Wheeling, and from there, the road goes across the Allegheny Mountains to Washington, Baltimore and Philadelphia. That route is all overland, a distance of 232 English miles — 358 on the river — but it was our intent to cross Lake Erie and travel through New York state from the west. We thus had to take a stagecoach north and wait for almost twenty-four hours for the first departure at eleven p.m. We had debarked at a nice Cincinnati hotel on the high river bank with the most beautiful view. After a dinner in the company of perhaps 200 travelers, I sat with several others outside the door to enjoy the clean air and the beautiful view when a small *barouche* with two stout horses stopped at the door. I first noted the words "Camp Meeting" written with chalk on the cart and assumed that the cart had been reserved by a traveler, but when nobody showed up and the driver started to address me, I soon learned that some four or five miles away there was a religious gathering of Methodists, who held public worship in the forest and had been there for a week, i.e., a camp meeting. The driver offered to take four of us for a piaster. Since I had a great inclination to get real knowledge of these fantastic gatherings, I talked several of the others into accompanying me and off we went.

The road through the richest clay soil was not of the best, but the surroundings were nice. Hills and valleys, forests and fields continually changed before our eyes, when we were not forced to close them for the deadly dust. We finally reached the sacred forest, and pilgrims coming and going had long announced its proximity. I must here ask the readers to imagine our Deer Park: half-barricaded roads, among the trees, wagons with unhitched horses munching, merchants with all kinds of merchandise as witness that even here spiritual food was not enough, and finally, a double circle of tents, in the center of which was a rough-hewn speaker's stand surrounded by benches. Instead of a white clown, who would have looked good, a reverend preacher stood thundering toward a big gathering, mostly women, very well-dressed, but mostly very simply in black, untrimmed or wrinkled silk dresses.

I arrived just in time to hear the closing of the pious man's sermon, which was richly characterized by the mystical Methodist sect's teachings, which scares the life out of sinners by exaggerated pictures of hell and all of its devils and thus, through an over-active imagination, shakes the nerves of the listeners. God knows that our preacher was successful, and I have never witnessed a more scandalous performance; many women fainted; others danced around as if they were possessed, tore at their hats and hair and continued until they collapsed. Yet others jumped around as if they were mad and yelled and screamed, supported by their friends. It is difficult to imagine such madness among a class from which one should expect more enlightenment in a free country and that the authorities are unable to do anything to prevent such gatherings, which can only ruin many a sound and strong constitution and make fanatics and fools out of sensible women and girls. But that is not enough: not everyone in such a gathering of young and old comes to be edified, and many hide under the cape of piety the better to be able to set into action plans which have very little in common with the sermons, and which they would be unable to do somewhere else. But what can be done when parents lead their daughters there so that they can become excited by the Holy Spirit, and tell themselves that this takes place when their nerves are moved so strongly that they carry on like lunatics! And this despicable sect spreads more and more across the country and daily makes new converts!

When Christians and Protestants do not make better use of their minds, [they] let us not wonder why the wild people dance around their idols and believe that they are inspired by the great spirits. They act according to their feelings and raw conceptions — and what are the Methodists doing? These meetings take place throughout the country and are arranged by the preachers in order to raise money because each is paid by his congregation. During the duration of the meeting, there is preaching and singing almost the entire day, and for eight days, there is talk only about the Bible, grace and faith; what they are thinking about, however, is a wholly different question. I left these holy wolves and their sheep, pleased with my increased knowledge of humanity and my lasting and more strongly-based conviction that wherever there are foxes there is no shortage of geese to feed them.

On the attached map of Ohio, I have marked my route in red ink. Nothing special happened. The road was terrible, especially the last half, which was through heavy woods still inhabited by Indians and it was opened only a couple of years ago. It snakes around tree stumps, of which not a single one has been cleared, and since the soil is very rich, there is a hole opposite each root, and these can be so deep that I often wondered how the wagons and horses could absorb the bumps that almost broke our limbs. The coaches were actually quite comfortable and the horses the nicest and strongest one could imagine. Our night lodgings and regular meals were as good as one could expect in small wooden shacks in the deepest forest and many miles from civilization. It was in these houses that we saw women dressed in the latest fashion, some rather gauche, but others in good taste, indicating a better position in life.

It took us four days and nights to get from Cincinnati to Sandusky, a distance of about 200 English miles, and we were lucky enough not to upset even once. One should not be surprised at the bad condition of the roads in a new state where everything needs to be done, and the condition of the soil presents big difficulties. It is more remarkable to consider what has already been accomplished in such a large and wild country, and that there already are enough passengers so that daily post coaches can be driven with stages every two to 2½ Danish miles (nine to ten English miles) on this long stretch. If one compares this with what is done in our native country, where the government has its fingers in everything, and where a hundred kinds of chains paralyze developments in every branch of industry, then one can only cross oneself over how blind the people are, who, for the benefit of a few, force millions into physical, and even worse, intellectual dependency.

In Upper Sandusky, an Indian village, I saw my first savages in their own environment. There were many whites living among them and the association with them has been a considerable influence on their customs. They dress almost like the whites, and I met several who spoke English with a soft and pleasant accent. But by being exposed to the higher culture, they had regrettably also acquired its biggest vices, and the detestable gin has caused an untimely death for many. These are only the remnants of a large and mighty tribe that has been exterminated by gin rather than by weapons, and probably like their brethren, will soon be gone from this earth.

In the inns all the way through Ohio, there are books in which the traveler enters his name, and in the last column, he adds his political opinion regarding the president of the Union by entering the name of the one he would prefer. Here in Ohio, which is an opposition state, one almost always saw Henry Clay (whom I have already mentioned), but this is only a weak guideline to public opinion. I discovered that the year Jackson was elected by a large majority of votes, there was in one of these books almost always this note, Adams, who was the then president and the opponent of Jackson. I mention this only as an example of how freely in this lucky country one can express one's opinion about even the highest-ranking person without having to worry about being prosecuted. For one of his character and the republican principles and rules, General Jackson, however, did little honor by his elevation to president and disgracefully abused his power in that respect. As the chief executive, he can fire and appoint any of the officials of the *United States* (as opposed to those from the individual states, over whom he has no power), principally customs officers and postmasters, which run into the thousands. Scarcely had he been elected before all of those who had supported his election were rewarded with positions at the expense of *numerous* heads of families, who, without notice and without being able to demand a pension, were dismissed, either because they had voted against him or had not strongly enough supported his election. This proscription was carried out so far that a simple letter from an anonymous person accusing an official of having been against Jackson's election was sufficient to have him removed from his position.

I heard a strange example of this. In a small town along the Mississippi, where the job of postmaster was only a burden, a boy decided to write to the president that the local postmaster had been against his election, but that someone else, and here he gave a name of someone who did not exist, was a strong admirer and supporter, and as a reward for his zeal, he ought to have the job as postmaster. He then signed the letter with so many names taken from history that it should have opened the eyes of the recipient, but Jackson was so blind when it came to punishing his enemies that without seeking further information he sent a commission to the place, which then dismissed the postmaster, but the person who was to be rewarded could not, of course, be found. The position was so lowly that they were unable to find anyone in town who would accept it. They finally had to reinstate the same man, increasing his salary to get him to accept it. So many other appointments of similar unworthy persons were made that the Senate, which must confirm all appointments made by the president, later rejected many without debate.

During the summer, there is a daily steamship connection across Lake Erie from the city of Buffalo in New York to Detroit in the Michigan Territory and these stop in Sandusky and Cleveland to pick up passengers. The distance from Sandusky to Buffalo is almost 240 English miles, which takes about 24 hours to traverse. The lake has the clearest water one can imagine, and it was calm when we crossed. During the late war between England and North America, many naval battles took place here since both sides had many warships which tried to inflict as much damage as possible on each other. The American side had the most victories. Although Ohio is a new state, considerable work has been done to improve connections internally; among these, is a canal from Cincinnati to Dayton in order to bring the Miami River closer to a market for the ones living in its vicinity, as well as several good roads on both sides of Columbus, the capital. But the most significant public project is the canal that cuts through the entire state from Cleveland to Portsmouth and thus connects Lake Erie with the Ohio River. The merchandise of the state can thus go either north through the big New York Canal to the state of the same name or to the Ohio River and on down to New Orleans. This canal is not yet completely finished, but a part of it that is already in use and which ends in Cleveland has already shown what it will be able to do.

Buffalo, which is still called a village, has gained so much with the new Erie Canal, which flows for 363 English miles through the entire state of New York from west to east, that it now has no fewer than 16,000 inhabitants and is still growing. It is located at the Niagara River, twenty-one miles from the famous Niagara Falls, the terrific roar of which can be heard downtown. We arrived about 3:00 p.m., and at the landing place, we found an unbelievable number of representatives of various modes of transportation, all of whom passed out their business cards, so that, in a monarchy, one would almost have thought we were nobility and had favors to pass out. But this is a result of free competition which always benefits the public. Since we had enough time before nightfall to see the falls, we hired a coach with four horses and went there without delay. A couple of miles from Buffalo, the river forms a considerable island, which had become famous even in Europe due to a plan by a Jewish Noah in New York to establish a New Jerusalem on it, and to that end had sent out a proclamation to his co-religionists recommending that they come there from all corners of the world to help him re-establish the temple. I recall having read this proclamation in Holland, where his plan did not find more adherents than it did elsewhere. The ardor of this prophet, no less honorable than many of his predecessors, did not cool down until it was pointed out to him that his holy land was right on the border of the American and English possessions and thus, in case of a new war, it ran the risk of being desecrated. It is unknown whether it was the thought of such a sin or his nation's natural respect for gunpowder that influenced the man, but enough about that; he gave up his plan, and instead, the high priest of Jerusalem settled for a lucrative position in New York State which his support of Jackson had secured for him.

We were getting close to perhaps the most uplifting show of nature on this earth, and already, every time the coach stopped, a distant thunder announced that it was near. The river current became furious, and the foam on the surface was witness to the speed at which it hit the exposed rocks. Nobody dares cross it here; an Indian who attempted it in his boat was carried away by the current and tumbled over the falls and his remains were never found. About two hundred fathoms above the falls, the river is perhaps 400 to 500 fathoms wide and *there*, strangely enough, it divides into two branches, leaving a sizable island in the middle, thereby forming two waterfalls, one on the English and the other on the American side. The island belongs to the Americans, who have finally succeeded with much difficulty in building a bridge across that branch of the river, fifty fathoms from the falls where the water is already, with enormous power, roaring down the already steep riverbed toward the fall. We arrived too late in the evening to be able to see the waterfall, and I must admit that I had difficulty reining in my curiosity. A very nice inn was a good indication of the many travelers who came to see this natural wonder. They number in the thousands every year. Most of the foreigners take lodging on the Canadian side, where two excellent hotels are located so that one can see both falls from their windows, which is not the case on the American side.

Niagara Falls

E arly in the morning of August 15, we went about two hundred fathoms down a spiral staircase to the foot of the falls, and it was a beautiful sight! This one, the American fall, has a perfect shape, as if it had been cut by a compass, and the water falls from a height of 170 feet (just like an enormous sheet gliding over a stick) but is majestic beyond all description and roaring so that it was almost impossible to make oneself understood. A heavy mist as from boiling water, formed by the extraordinary power with which the river poured down, almost blocked the sight of the English fall at the place where we stood, although there were only the above-mentioned island and the rock wall on which it rests between the two. Although the distance from the island to the American side was several hundred fathoms and twice that distance from the English fall, the water was so rough that it appeared foolhardy to go there in a boat. A regularly scheduled ferry with a dinghy contradicted this, and the only unpleasant part of the crossing was a violent dancing, while the view was enchanting. It is too sublime to permit my non-poetic pen to even give a shadow of a description of a scene, the observance of which impresses the spirit more than it does the senses, and many could feel it but few describe it. I will therefore, like a theatrical bungler, fling out a few colors and leave it to the imagination of the audience to create other than splotches out of it.

The valley through which the Niagara River rushes is surrounded by high rock walls on all sides which have some brush and forest growing but are very steep. There are houses all around on the top, especially on the English side, where I am right now. The view is as picturesque as can be, although it is not only the eye, but also the ear that is influenced; an artist's brush could never convey an appropriate impression of this. The English fall is broader than the American and carries more water, but it is not as regular. It is approximately 100 fathoms wide and is in the shape of a horseshoe, and the water falling from it is so deep that it maintains its green color until it mixes with the foam at the foot. Clouds of steam rise far above the top of the fall and show all the colors of the rainbow when there is even the least bit of sunshine. I was not fortunate enough to experience that kind of weather, and the view is so extraordinary and enthralling that I was sorry that I only had a few hours to watch it; one could spend days and even weeks without getting tired of it. The view changes almost every hour of the day with the light having such an influence, and in order to fully enjoy it, one should not neglect seeing it at sunrise, and sunset and by moonlight. I was now close to the frightful waterfall on a flat rock, called Table Rock, that juts out and from which it is impossible to look down without fear of tumbling down in an immeasurable abyss from a height of 174 feet. Nearby is a spiral stairway down to a small house built up against the rock wall, and those who wish to go *under the fall* disrobe and go with a guide. This is a hair-raising undertaking, but it did not stop me, except that I was in a lather and did not have time to get undressed first. I just got closer to the cave and looked up at the fall, which, from this angle, had a strange effect. The earth shook under its unpredictable weight, and one's spirit trembles in its attempt to understand the incomprehensible. Many who are versed in natural science have made attempts to determine the quantity of water flowing over every minute, but everything must remain an estimate since it is unknown how deep the river is where it flows over the rock wall. But even with one's naked eyes one can see that millions of barrels must pass across in that time! The Niagara Falls is the only discharge from the Great Lakes of Superior, Huron, Michigan, and Erie, and then it flows through Lake Ontario and the St. Lawrence River, passing Quebec in Hudson Bay [sic].

From the above-mentioned island on the American side of the fall, a bridge has been built out on protruding rocks, and from its head, where there are some benches, one can see straight down into the foaming and roaring abyss, and one has to convince oneself that the bridge is solid before daring go out thereon. I could sit there for hours just staring at this unbelievable wonder and think about the unending powers of God and Nature. It would be interesting to know how deep into the ground this falling water has gone after these many centuries, but even here the most knowledgeable minds are unable to make any estimates. Several experiments have been done, but mainly to satisfy the curiosity of the masses and to entice people to come to the inns, and they have been successful in that respect. Among other things, someone built a boat and on it was loaded a bear, a fox and some geese, and then it was let flow with the current and over the falls. The geese flew away, but the boat and the other animals have never been seen since. The Niagara and its falls flow thus:

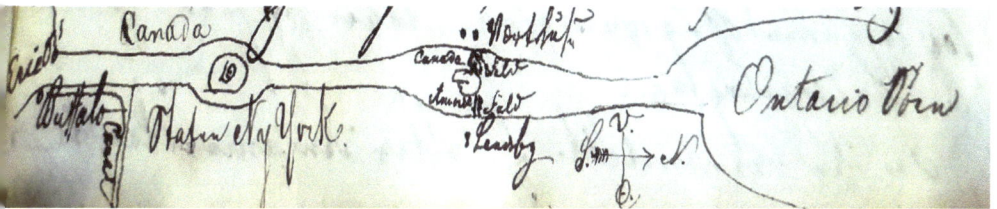

Rudolph's Rendering of Niagara Falls' Flow

From Niagara, which will always have a special place in my memories, we returned to the canal on which we were to travel through the state of New York. This mode of travel is both comfortable and inexpensive and almost as speedy as the stage coach, since the Americans, although many in this state are descendants of the Dutch, are not stuck in a rut as were their honorable ancestors. While they go at a snail's pace on the Dutch canals with boats they used 200 years ago, everything here is arranged for speed and comfort. All meals are taken on the boats, and at night the seats are arranged as beds so one can spend the night just as one would at home. The boats are pulled by three horses, which trot right along, and this covers the 364 miles in no more than three nights and days, even though we had to go through eighty locks. In Holland, such a trip would have taken at least fourteen days! This wonderful project, which cost millions, was completed in spite of the most immense opposition, which even brought out the rabble to threaten the life of the governor De Wito Clintou [DeWitt Clinton—transl.], who by virtue of his strong willpower, brought the project to its completion. They are now in the process of honoring him, since this canal connecting the west, so rich in products, with the ocean, has brought such treasures down to New York, which alone is the launching place for them and the goods which are sent back in return. The canal itself pays such significant taxes to the state, that in just a few years it will have paid for itself. In 1830, the duties on this and the other canals in the state will bring in over one million piasters to the public purse!

The difficulties that had to be overcome in order to complete this wonderful project are extraordinary, and one has to admire the genius who drew up the plans through an absolutely wild country of mountains, rivers and valleys. Near Lockport, the first city we passed through, there were some surprising projects going on. Above the city, they had to blast through a mountain for a stretch of several miles, and in the city itself, two rows of locks with five in each have also been blasted, so two boats can go up and down at the same time at an elevation of sixty-odd feet, which separates the surface of the water above and below the locks. This project deserves the highest praise; it is built in a way that does not show any unjust rush or stinginess, which cannot be said about all of the locks, many of which are already in need of considerable maintenance (the canal is only seven–eight years old). This canal has an extended life expectancy along its entire length of 380 English miles (almost eighty Danish miles), and there are already many cities and villages along it. Before it was built, there were no towns and just a few villages. The first city of any size that we came to was Rochester, with over 16,000 inhabitants and many factories, especially flour mills, which are driven by the water from a swift river flowing under the canal by means of a beautiful water pipe; it forms a 100-foot high waterfall near the city. The waterfall is beautiful when the water level in the river is high, but it did not make a big impression on me now, and especially after having seen the Niagara. The other towns we passed through were very nice: all new construction and painted and bearing witness to industry and wealth. There were still many tree stumps in some streets, and all over there was a dearth of gardens, which I feel is a necessity. Only the names of these small towns could be interesting to my readers and me since they are almost all from ancient history. We thus came through Palmyra, Syracuse, Rome, Troy, and Utica as well as Lyon, Amsterdam, Montezuma, and so on. Maybe some day these new cities will overshadow the ones from history! But hardly in war and conquests.

The landscape along the canal is constantly changing, and in many places, the view is enchanting; the canal itself sometimes goes through several-hundred-foot high banks and sometimes over seventy-foot dikes, but it is especially after it joins the bed of the Mohawk River, which flows through a mountainous part of the state, that one would never tire of the beautiful view that Nature offers. The village of Little Falls, where the buildings mainly consist of large factories built of stone and are located between the mountains where the river drops through, is especially picturesque.

Since I had to be in New York before the packet-boat left for Le Havre on August 20, I was prevented from taking a side trip to Saratoga's warm mineral springs, the American Pyrmont, where the elite from the United States and many from Canada spend a few weeks every summer and which is located only 40 English miles from Albany, a considerable city by the Hudson River and the capital of the state of New York. I would also have liked to make a short stop here, but we arrived just as the steamboat gave its last departure signal, and it was too important for me to pass down the beautiful Hudson River during the day that I had no thought but of getting aboard. I therefore just took a glimpse at the town as I passed through. It was established by the Dutch almost 150 years ago and has about 30,000 inhabitants and much commerce, especially since the canal was built. We passed the palace of the legislative powers, and it seemed worthy of its purpose.

The distance from Albany is 145 English miles, a trip that would have taken five to eight days before the invention of the steamboat but which now can be done in twelve hours! There are three regularly scheduled daily passenger boats back and forth, plus many at irregular hours, and these boats are nice and powerful. One can get an idea of the unbelievable number of travelers on the Hudson River when one realizes that those steamships going three times daily during the summer seldom carry fewer than 200 passengers and often 500 to 600 passengers each. They take their meals aboard and the ones traveling at night sleep on the boats. The boat *North America* has two separate engines, each about eighty horsepower, and each driving its wheel, which gives it an exceptional speed. It felt as if we were flying through the air and water, and now they are building a competing boat on a different principle. It is named *South America* and promises to make the 145-mile trip in nine hours.

The Hudson is the most beautiful river I have ever seen, and there is probably not another like it in the whole world. It has very few bends and flows through very high country with mountains in the distance, and only hills along the river that constantly change in height and appearance. Almost all are overgrown or tilled and there are many houses, villages and cities on both sides. I was very excited about this view, the beauty and richness of which one cannot imagine. West Point, the United States Army Cadet Academy, is located by itself on a high hill ninety-three English miles from New York. They train very capable officers here, and it is hard to understand why the navy does not have something similar; its officers are only trained onboard ship just as they are in England and thus, most often are without any social or scientific education outside their ship. I doubt if they learn as much as the captains of our mercantile fleet.

In approaching a famous city, I believe it is impossible to not make for oneself an idea of its appearance, which usually far surpasses reality. This was not the case with St. Petersburg, which was far beyond my conception. I cannot say the same about New York. To judge a city's prosperity, one should probably consider its private buildings and, in a republic, neither expect the luxuriant palaces of a rich aristocracy nor the stamp of a despotic royal power's contempt for the sweat of the people nor treasures in monuments or castles. Yet for Europeans who grew up with such prejudices, it is difficult to imagine a wealthy city without combining the concept of what we are used to, considering the necessary indications and, as in all other things, combining the known with the unknown. In that respect, the first view of New York does not please the European who has visited some of the world's prime locations. But he must be considered both mindless and heartless who feels nothing upon closer consideration of a Newness, where everything is life, moving in order, prosperity and freedom. We checked into the large North American Hotel, which has 200 rooms and so many guests that we had to share three to a room. The restaurants are well kept, the rooms are richly furnished, and the food is excellent. But with the large number of travelers who can afford to pay high prices, it is quite probable that everyone gets rich who can get over the initial costs of establishment.

New York City, New York

New York has the most excellent location for trade any city can have. It was established 200 years ago by the Dutch, who knew how to do things, and it was called Nieuw Amsterdam. The English, who are not stupid in that respect either, took it away from them fifty years later and renamed it after the king's brother, the Duke of York, and kept it until the colonies won their independence in 1783. From that era stems the beginning of the city's extraordinary growth in population and wealth that has already elevated it to the leading city in the New World with more than 210,000 inhabitants and the State of New York approximately two million. Its trade and shipping to all corners of the world is unbelievable, and if it keeps increasing — which everything shows signs of doing — it will soon become a second Venice and Genoa and defy the leading commercial centers of Europe.

Besides the numerous splendid restaurants, there are also many so-called boardinghouses, or private homes, where families and single men can board and room and live in a family setting, which especially for the ladies is much more pleasant. Many of these houses are very stylish, and the prices are as high as at the restaurants, usually eight to ten piasters per week (seventy-five to eighty-five Rbdl. [=Danish *rigsbanksdaler*] per month). All other prices are comparable, and nobody should come to America for economic reasons. I did find a cheaper and quite nice house later at six piasters per week. Inland the cost of living except for clothing is much lower, and in a city in Indiana (New Albany), which I have already mentioned, one can find room and board in a good inn for two piasters a week.

In New York, there are no fewer than 114 churches and chapels of a score of some twenty different sects and denominations and, in religiosity, the Americans do not short anything that might be said about the piety of their ancestors, be they English or Batavians. Their Sundays, when the truly pious families neither receive visitors nor go anywhere other than to church, and no public amusements or even public reading-rooms are open, are unbelievably boring to a foreigner. Until recently, the sermons in many churches were still held in Dutch. Now, only the names "Dutch Reformed," and *Huys des Heeren* and other similar inscriptions on the church walls bear witness to the people who established them because everything is in English, both the church service and their language, in which quite Dutch names suggest their origin, and, of them, there are many.

There is not much entertainment suited for those who come from the European capitals, and they only distinguish themselves by being expensive. There are two far from large, but nicely appointed, theaters which have daily shows of the same caliber as the ones in New Orleans, which I have described earlier, and I only visited them infrequently. During the winter, there are balls and concerts that are not any better than the ones in Europe. There was an Italian opera here for a couple of years, but it was unable to make a go of it, although it had several good talents, among them the famous Mad. Mahbran. The French troupe from New Orleans comes now to the northern theaters every summer and is doing quite well.

On September 4, reports came to New York about the French revolution and caused much excitement and not so little enthusiasm among the many French-born and French descendants here. The immortal Marseillaise was sung at the theaters where the Tricolor was worn on many hats, and it caused an excitement that I had not expected to witness on any occasion, and it gave me an idea of how it must have been in France. Even the

Americans showed much sympathy, although being half Dutch and half English, their blood by nature is very thick and thus, is harder to move, especially at events that do not touch them directly.

New York is built on a tongue of land formed by the Hudson River on one side and the so-called East River, which is actually just an arm of the sea that separates Long Island from the mainland, on the other side. Nature could never have created a more beautiful harbor, which is surrounded by a rocky landscape and with water deep enough to accommodate the heaviest ships. And being sheltered by the high country on all sides, no harbor could be more protected against wind and weather. The view from the point of the land that, even after having been converted to a walking path, still bears the name of Battery, is absolutely beautiful, and the high islands surrounding the harbor are well-planted and full of houses and amusement parks. On several of them are entrenchments above which fly the beautiful American flag, and most of them are close enough that one can see even small objects.

The city of Brooklyn on Long Island is just across from New York and has no fewer than 13,000 inhabitants. The distance between the two is no greater than the one from Amager to Copenhagen where they are connected by Langebro, and there, most of the amusement places for wealthy New Yorkers are located. However, they are not distinguished by taste or splendor. The exceptional depth of the river and the heavy traffic upon it, which would be hindered by a bridge, has prevented its construction, and instead, the traffic is handled by three ferryboat companies, which every ten minutes have boats leaving from both sides. New York harbor also has the advantage that shipping is seldom stopped by ice, which is the case in Philadelphia and Baltimore, although they are at the same, more southerly latitude as Rome and Naples. This difference in climate on the two continents is extremely strange. New York, at a latitude of 41° and thus, even with Florence and Barcelona, has a winter almost like ours, and in New Orleans, which is even with Cairo in Egypt, they sometimes have thick ice during the winter, and orange trees and other tender trees are killed. The difference is attributed to the large lakes and the untilled expanses of land although it is hard to give a reason for this, especially since later winters, where more land has been cultivated than ever before, have been more severe than many before.

On September 28, I left New York for a visit to Philadelphia, Baltimore and Washington. The flow of travelers here is maybe even heavier than between New York and Albany, and the mode of transportation is not less comfortable although some of the trip is overland. The distance between New York and Philadelphia is ninety-seven English miles, which is covered in ten or eleven hours, so that by leaving at six or seven in the morning — and steamships depart both hours — the entire trip is done during daylight. However, this speed is nothing compared to what it will be when the new railroad is completed that has been started between Camden, outside Philadelphia, and Amboy, twenty-three English miles from New York. One should be able to eat lunch in New York, stay for three–four hours in Philadelphia and be back before evening. These railroads are marvels, and nothing is thus more natural than the fact that the Americans, who do not have to wait for either favor or grace or fight against privileges or taxes, build them wherever it is reasonable that they will be profitable, and there is hardly a state where they do not plan on building these roads in order to ease the transportation connections, and it is unbelievable how easy it is for money to be raised.

The stretch of New Jersey that we passed through is not very beautiful; the soil is poor and we saw mainly apple and pear trees and the people make their living mainly by preparing juices which are sold far and wide. Near Trenton, a very famous city from the American Revolution, we passed a country estate where the great and unfortunate General Moreau spent many years, only leaving it to join the enemies of the land of his birth, which cost him his life. Only the outbuildings are still standing after a fire burned down the residence. In Bordentown, a couple of miles from Trenton, Joseph Bonaparte owns a place, called Point Briere, where the main building has suffered the same fate as that of Moreau's. It burned down during his absence, and he lost many excellent paintings and other reminders of his former high status. He has now converted the stables into a residence, and where it used to stand and where there is a magnificent view of the Delaware River and all the half-uncultivated land, he has built a wooden belvedere eighty to 100 feet high which can be seen from afar. Joseph Bonaparte is very hospitable and allows everyone to view his property; his secretary was even kind enough to let me see his beautiful collection of paintings and marble busts of members of his family, most of which had been sculpted by Canova.

Among his paintings were several by David depicting scenes from Napoleon's life that have become known all over the world as copperplates. A life-size portrait of himself in Spanish royal garb hangs in his dining room, and the sight of it reminded me of an actor who had been hissed off the stage playing Hamlet. He is otherwise sensible enough to lead a simple life and not put on airs in his circle, the opposite would cause ridicule here, which was the case when in a letter he recently wrote to General Lallemand [and which was published], and expressed some kind of protest against the appointment of the Duke of Orleans as king because Napoleon had passed on the crown to his son, and he (Joseph) was the head of the family. Thank God that the French nation will not be subjected to the head or tail of this family. Otherwise, they would soon get a civil war started, which would aid them and other hungry wolves to assume new roles in the bloody drama that would then be played out.

The appearance of Philadelphia was even less pleasing to me than New York, although it had been described to me as the most beautiful city in the new world. Since I had seen Mexico, I had naturally elevated my opinions a couple of steps, but in reality, I was forced to lower them at least ten. The streets are straight and of a nice width and several had a row of trees on each side and were usually very clean. But instead of the big massive stone buildings with balconies and archways and the numerous churches and monasteries with their magnificent towers and domes that one would see in the streets of Mexico City, Philadelphia offered only narrow two- to three-story middle-class houses, all of which were painted red with white chalk stripes, and had a stone stoop with a railing and frequently white-painted exterior shutters on the windows that looked disgusting. There were also more than eighty churches, but only two had tolerable towers, and almost all were built in a poor and tasteless style. I have difficulty understanding how this can be compared with, and even preferred, over Mexico City unless the people in both cities are figured in, and here the difference, although on the opposite side, is much bigger.

One must also understand that in public institutions Philadelphia is far superior to Mexico City, where the priests and monks are in charge while here they are managed by people who are the descendants of the ones who gave the city its pretty name, "brotherly love."

Philadelphia now has 167,000 inhabitants and is growing at a rate similar to that of its sister cities, although not as rapidly as New York. In internal improvements and projects, Pennsylvania is not behind its neighboring states, and railroads and canals are expanding in all directions to ease transportation connections to various parts. Of public works in the city, the waterworks especially deserves to be mentioned. It supplies the entire city with excess water up to the top floors of the buildings. A dam on the Schuylkill River (which flows behind the city and has excellent water) elevates the water level sufficiently to drive a water-wheel, which operates several pumps, moving the water into tanks up to seventy to eighty feet; from here, it flows through trenches all through the city. This project is impressive and is so ingenious in planning and construction. The new penitentiary [reformatory] is built in a great Gothic style on the principle of solitary confinement. It bears witness to the degree of perfection that prisons have come to in America, and one can only wonder why their good results have not opened the eyes of other governments, which have been successful in punishing but hardly in reforming their criminals.

The United States Bank is a noble building completely in the style of a Greek temple, but its exterior is so striking that its very tasteful, although proportionally it's not quite sufficiently elevated interior loses all effect at first viewing. Also, the new Pennsylvania Bank building and Stephen Girard's Bank are of a beautiful design. The latter is solely owned by Mr. Stephen Girard; he is a man whose wealth cannot easily be estimated, but it could be from fifteen to twenty million piasters! There is no doubt that he is the biggest mystery in Philadelphia. He is over eighty years old and still manages his bank and all his other extensive enterprises, which are spread all over the earth. He was born in Bordeaux and by going to sea when he did not own two nickels to rub together, and he has worked himself up to being probably the wealthiest merchant on earth. He never married and, although he is very benevolent, he will have nothing to do with his relatives, who ignored him when he was in trouble. His feelings in that regard are so strong that his sister, who came to America a couple of years ago to visit him before she died, had to return without seeing him. The city of Philadelphia will probably receive the majority of his wealth for worthy foundations. I was introduced to him, but due to his high age, it was difficult to carry on a regular conversation with him.

Between Philadelphia and Baltimore, a distance of 120 English miles, and from there to the capital of the United States, Washington (thirty-seven miles), there are just as many travelers as between Philadelphia and New York. Between the two first-mentioned cities, there are two or three steamships daily and horse-boats along the canal, which goes through the bit of land that bisects Delaware. This canal is eighteen miles long and in places cuts through seventy to eighty-foot high banks and over dams of almost the same height. The entire distance is covered in eleven to twelve hours.

Baltimore is a city of no fewer than 80,000 inhabitants and, with an extensive trade, especially with South America, whence it ships much flour and other provisions. In order to get products from the western states without going through New Orleans, the way it does now, the entrepreneurial citizens have decided to build a railway to the Ohio River, a distance of over 300 English miles. The difficulties they are facing are so extraordinary that each of the thirteen miles they have completed so far has cost 50,000 piasters! Nonetheless, the city and the State of Maryland have been able to do this work without assistance from the government, but it is certain that if it does not live up to the hopes and expectations of everyone, half of Baltimore will be ruined since all of its citizens have shown that much interest in its completion. National liberty creates national spirit!

To travel by railroad is almost like traveling on a level stone floor, and the friction is so slight that one horse can run fast pulling a load of fifty to sixty passengers, which on the best road would require at least six horses. Although the thirteen-mile long Baltimore railroad has been very expensive to build, it is also a wonderful project, passing through the mountains and across rivers and deep valleys. There are two tracks almost the entire distance, and the bed is laid on a base of rock. A similar project between Le Havre and Paris and Hamburg and Lybeck could mean a gold-mine to those undertaking it. In France, this would be impossible right now, but without regulation, and God save Denmark from that, such undertakings could probably never get started across its territory. During the last four months, sightseers alone have provided the Baltimore Company an income in excess of 100,000 piasters, although they only charge 37½ cents for the thirteen-mile trip, but the major road from south to north passes through Baltimore. During the four summer months, half of America's wealthy families, especially from the southern states, spend their time in inns, stage coaches and steamships. A 245-foot-high white marble column with a gigantic statue on top has recently been built to the memory of [George] Washington, the great American hero. It is very tastefully done by an Italian artist. [Possibly a reference to the Washington Monument in Baltimore, designed by American architect Robert Mills].

Washington, the capital, is only thirty-seven miles from Baltimore, separated by a very poor, sandy stretch of land. Almost every hour of the day, there is a stage coach going between the two cities, but the Baltimore Railway Company has secured permission to construct a branch of their road there and, in the future, that will naturally become the only mode of transportation. The great Capitol, where the legislature meets, is the first thing one notices when one approaches Washington, just as it is the first building one passes, although, according to the original plan, it is located in the center of the city. But Washington, which is planned to have 200,000–300,000 inhabitants, still has only 18,000 residents. Its location is not as favorable for trade as its neighboring cities, so without trade, no growth.

The populated part of the city is toward the west, and at its outer point is the president's house (palace is too monarchical an expression), a rather large two-story sandstone building, completely isolated and surrounded by fields, which are probably planned for gardens but strangely enough are completely bare. The house itself looks very republican. Some pillars in a semicircle at the main entrance and a double spiral staircase on the opposite façade seemed to me to be of a poor taste. The Capitol, on the other hand, is in a sublime style built by an Italian and worthy of its purpose. It consists of a main building with a large dome (230 feet above sea level and 180 above its base), and two wings, in one of which the Senate is located, and in the other, the House of Representatives. The dome itself forms a magnificent hall with eight large paintings depicting the American War of Independence, but only four have been completed. This entrance is too majestic for comparison with the rest and the important, namely the other meeting halls, which in taste were inferior to that which I have seen in Holland and France, and even in Mexico. The exterior of the building, which is located on a hill, is impressive, and both façades are decorated with many columns in a magnificent style.

I did not see President Jackson, although I was God-fearing enough to go to church just to meet him. He is an old man, aged 70 years, tall and skinny and ugly as a revenant, and — as his opponents say — without the slightest talent for governance. He nonetheless has many followers, and no matter how mighty his opposition is, he will probably be reelected president next year. I could write much about the terrible strife between the two parties, and which will probably develop into something other than a battle of pens and allocations, but my book is singing its last verse, and I must use the few pages left to me for other than speculative items.

I was back in New York at the beginning of November, and on the 26th, was the celebration of the French revolution, the like of which had only been seen on the occasion of the dedication of the great Erie Canal. On such occasions where nothing is demanded, but everything was voluntary, the free arrangements show their best side. Some ordinary citizens called a meeting in the newspapers of those who would contribute to celebrating the French revolution and invited ex-president Monroe to chair the meeting. It was also decided to invite the city and state's civilian and military authorities, the militia, and all the trades and businesses to take part in the celebration. Committees were appointed to organize all of it, and thus, the process got started without any interference by the authorities; about 25,000 residents participated. It must have cost the working classes several hundred thousand piasters since they all sacrificed one full day's work besides paying for considerable tri-colored decorations, which could be seen all over. The parade was at least three to four miles long, and in it was everything the city and the State of New York owned of distinction. One should hope that they may never regret their participation in the liberation of a people who greatly contributed to the happy outcome of their own revolution.

Return to the South

There is nothing sadder than waiting for news and not knowing when it will arrive, but this longing becomes completely intolerable when important decisions rely on it and when they fail to come at a time one needs them the most and when it seems reasonable that they should be here. Those in America who are directly influenced by European information constantly feel this, but habit is everything, and I who did not possess it thus suffered extremely in this period so unusual for Europe. As early as November, I had expected letters every day, the contents of which would decide whether I should stay in New York or make the long trip down to New Orleans. Not until December 20, did a ship bring it to me and already on December 22, I was aboard the packet ship *Niagara* headed for Charleston in South Carolina. We set sail on the 23rd, but unfortunately with a headwind which did not leave us, and on a journey which especially at this time of the year only takes three to four days, it took us fifteen! The company onboard was not of the best, but the living conditions were very good, and with the exception of a couple of days of seasickness and the unavoidable heat, combined with the lack of desire for and an opportunity to occupy myself, I have good reason to be happy about this trip at sea. In Charleston, which is located at 32 degrees 40 minutes, I expected the same climate as the preceding year in New Orleans, but found that it could not possibly have been worse if my trip had been as many degrees northwards.

The worst part was that the houses are adapted for the summer and in that respect are better looking and practical than the buildings in New Orleans. Charleston is a nice city with 30,000 inhabitants and a good harbor and from here is exported much cotton and that wonderful Carolina rice, which is raised close-by. It can only grow there because in order for the seed to thrive, the field must be flooded after the seed is planted and must remain that way for a long period of time, and then it needs strong heat. Both can be accomplished here since the vicinity of Charleston is low-lying and boggy, and also so unhealthy that even the native-born are unable to stay there during the hottest summer months without risking dying from the fever. *They* are safe in town, but foreigners cannot even stay there and have to go to a small island just outside or simply leave the state, which is the safest thing to do. I attended the celebration of the anniversary of Charleston's railroad. This is the road that leads to Augusta in Georgia (almost 150 English miles), where much of the cotton comes from which is shipped out from Charleston. It goes along the river, which means of transportation is much slower and more expensive, and at the start of *the season* (which starts October 1) also completely impossible with the low water level of the river. There is a fear that it will mean a decline for the city of Savannah when the road is completed in a few years. Only a distance of about ten miles has been completed and that is across boggy land much of the way, with the entire stretch resting on poles that are rammed down in the soil so that the track is three feet and sometimes more above the surface. Since the cars are set in motion by a steam-car, the road is not filled in the center but is absolutely open. We were about 110 passengers traveling almost six miles in 25 minutes, and the steam-car pulled us without any effort!

I stayed in Charleston for two weeks, and there I encountered young Hambro from Copenhagen with whom I became acquainted in Le Havre before I left for America, and whom I had since met in New York. He is a person who does not disgrace his country no matter how little sympathy he seemed to have for it, and whom I would always be happy to meet again. His intent was to go down to New Orleans and go back north the same route I came last year.

Savannah, 114 miles from Charleston, is located on a high sandy hill on the river of the same name and has only 7,000 inhabitants but has a considerable export of cotton and rice, and there were several large ships in its harbor. The streets are very regular and have trees planted on both sides, but there is no pavement and one wades in sand everywhere. In order to lessen the deadly influence of the sun, the streets are very wide with many open squares. The very nice houses, usually surrounded by gardens, are built far from each other, and all in all, it looks like a big, beautiful village. The Presbyterian church is the most beautiful I have seen in America, but its nice tower and Dorian pillars look strange in an ocean of sand. Their hospitality is great, and a stranger who has been recommended to someone from the first families is assured that he will not be having many dinners alone.

After a few days' stay in Savannah, the beautiful steamboat *David Mongin* brought me to Augusta, a distance of 138 English miles. The river is not remarkable; it meanders like the Mississippi, and its wild, uncultivated banks call back memories. Augusta, with 6,000 inhabitants, is the main mercantile town in the state of Georgia, and while I was there, they had no fewer than 50,000 bales of cotton in the warehouses. Although it is built in the same style as Savannah, it is not nearly as pretty. It has the appearance of a commercial city, and several fires in later years have had the same effect on it as the 1795 and 1807 fires had on Copenhagen.

Here, the comfortable part of my trip is ended, and my trials now started; 460 miles across the State of Georgia, the territory of the savages and the half-wild state of Alabama lay before me. I knew that the roads were terrible, but I must admit that I was not prepared to find them [in] such an unbelievably and indescribably bad condition as was the case. And when one thinks about the stage coaches going through with the mail three times every week, night and day, it becomes a new test of everything in a free country being possible, where *the absolute master,* namely *the people*, reap the benefits. So far, it has not been possible to construct good roads on this immense and almost unpopulated stretch, and it will, of out of necessity, take many years. During the summer months, these roads are very good, since the many boggy areas and streams one sometimes has to wade through and swim across are dry and level as a floor. It is fortunate that the good season here lasts from April till November.

After six days and seven nights of bumping and getting through a thousand dangers, and threats of upsets and the breaking of arms and legs through a too long stretch of land only inhabited by savages, I arrived tired and chilled in the town of Mobile on the Gulf of Mexico and a one-day trip from New Orleans. This is Alabama's only harbor, and although the town has only 5,000–6,000 inhabitants, it exported over 100,000 bales of cotton last year. The town, as well as the state, is growing, and in the future, it could get to play an important role. It is so cold that one would think that one was 'way up north; I had never thought it could be this cold at 30° latitude.

Mobile did not offer anything unique, and I just stayed for a few days. I yearned for New Orleans, where I had left so many friends and acquaintances, and I rushed off and arrived here already on February 9 after having traveled a couple of thousand Danish miles (x 4.68 = over 9000 English miles) since I left last year.

I will hereby close my diary of a trip, which by a more skilled and better trained pen than mine would be able to furnish material for several tomes. But reading it incomplete as it is, might possibly offer a few hours of diversion to my loved ones, and in later years, help me to recall the events, which will forever be an important and pleasant part of my life. And that is its only purpose.

- - - - - - - -

P.S. I have learned here that the money escort from Mexico City to Real del Monte was attacked and plundered by robbers after a hard-fought battle in which the English had to yield to a superior force, and after my friend McIntosh had been severely wounded.

Rudolph's Letter Requesting U.S. Citizenship and Receipt for Paid Fare Aboard the Ship, *Hunter*

Rudolph's Watch
Purchased for his mother. It is still in the family today.

NOTICE.—The subscribers have entered into a limited partnership, pursuant to the first title of the fourth chapter of the second part of the Revised Statutes of the State of New York, on the following terms :—The name or firm of the said partnership is R. BRAEM. The general nature of the business intended to be transacted by it, is Mercantile—consisting of the purchase and sale of merchandise, and Commission and other agency business. The subscriber, Rudolph Braem, is the general partner, and the other subscribers are the special partners in the said partnership. The said special partners have contributed to the common stock of the said partnership, in cash payments, the following sums—that is to say, Alexander H. Monod the sum of twenty-five hundred dollars; Edouard A. Monod the further sum of twenty-five hundred dollars, and Alexandre J. T. Sanson Davillier the further sum of five thousand dollars. The said partnership commences on the first day of April, 1836, and will terminate on the first day of April, 1846.

Dated this nineteenth day of March, A. D. 1836.

R. BRAEM,
A. H. MONOD,
E. A. MONOD,
A. J. T. SANSON DAVILLIER.

March 29, 1836. law6w

Notice Published in the *New York Post*
Announcing the Opening of Rudolph's Company,
Effective April 1, 1836

21.

Warren Co., Va. 21st ult Mrs Martha Randolph wid of Beverly Officer of Rev. and among the first Governors of the State

Wednesday, October 10, 1838.

Tues Oct.9, Susan Jane dau of Edmund and Susan Anderson 14y 2m. Remains Greenwich for interment. 61 Hester St

Tues Emily A Van Anden dau of Henry and Emily. brother in law Charles Hunter. 125 Hester St

Tues Jane w Ellis Price in 55y 14 Oak St

Thurs. Elizabeth w Chester Johnson, 41-9-4, decd. was formerly from Hudson N Y 29 First St

Monday John Hulna, of Shrewsburg, England, late of Manhattan 10 Frankfort St

Tues Samuel R son of James and Margaret Ann Tisdale, 2-4-5

Tues Elizabeth Elliot dau of William B Coles in 4y 82 Laight

Tues in 80th yr Robert Allwood, Judge Supreme Court of Judicature and member of Assembly of Jamaica, W I

Oct 7 Alonzo only child of Alonzo A & Susan Alvord in 1y

Bristol, Ulster Co., Oct 3, in 35th yr Amelia A w of Rev J Judson Buck and dau of late Charles Duryee of this City

Thursday, October 11, 1838.

This morning in 38y Jacob C Cauldwell of this City borther in law Thomas Cook. 64 Mulberry St

Wed John Mackay 74yrs son John, Jr. 50 Walker St St. Johns Ch

Choctaw Agency 30th ult Mingo Mushulatubee, 60yrs

Marcelus, Onondaga Co NY Dan Bradley, 71yrs

Friday, October 12, 1838

Thurs Oct 11, Rudolph Braem in 38th yr Henry St Bklyn

Oct 11, Charles Maison in 37y brother in law Wm Seymour. 7 Lispenard St

Wed Anne Carter inf dau of Adam P and Jane T Pentz

Wed Oct 10, nr Hackensack NJ Peter A Kipp, 56y

Saturday, October 13, 1838.

Oct.12, Nancy M Ransom, 20y brother J.H. 109-2nd St

Friday res. of D Clay, 130 Franklin St Rev A C Morgan, 36 of Waterbury, Conn

Rudolph's Death Notice

THE

People of the State of New-York,

BY THE GRACE OF GOD, FREE AND INDEPENDENT:

To all to whom **THESE PRESENTS SHALL COME**, or may concern,

SEND GREETING:

Know Ye, That at the City of Brooklyn _____ in the County of Kings, on the eighteenth _____ day of November October in the year of our Lord one thousand eight hundred and thirty eight _____ before Richard Cornwell, Esquire, Surrogate of our said County, the last Will and Testament of Rudolph G. s Braem late of the City of Brooklyn in the County of Kings _____

deceased, (a copy whereof is hereunto annexed,) was proved, and is now approved and allowed by us; and the said deceased at or immediately previous to his death was an Inhabitant of the said County of Kings _____

by reason whereof the proving and registering the said Will and the granting Administration of all and singular the goods, chattels, and credits, of the said deceased, and also the auditing, allowing, and final discharging the account thereof, doth belong unto the Surrogate of the said County: the administration of all and singular the goods, chattels and credits of the said deceased, and any way concerning his Will, is granted unto Felix Collomb in conjunction with Elizabeth M Braem and Obadiah Holmes to whom Letters Testamentary were heretofore granted the surrogate of the County of Kings he being one of the _____

Executors in the said Will named and he being first duly sworn _____ faithfully and honestly to discharge the duties of such Executor _____

IN TESTIMONY WHEREOF, we have caused the Seal of Office of our said Surrogate to be hereunto affixed.

Witness, Richard Cornwell _____ Esquire, Surrogate of our said County, at the City of Brooklyn the Twentie Eighth _____ day

---

Rudolph's Last Will and Testament

Afterword

Shortly after Rudolph returned to France, he set sail for New York City in December 1832 to seek his fortune as a timber baron in America. The lumber industry was quickly growing at this time as forests were being cut at a dramatic pace, providing wood for building ships, homes, and businesses, as well as providing fuel for steam-powered engines in ferries and trains.

In March 1836, Rudolph started his own mercantile business, being backed by the Monod Brothers and Sanson Davillier. We have some old newspaper articles referencing the buying and selling of cotton and sugar. If you recall from his entries, Rudolph spent time in Savannah, Georgia, and one must assume he made contacts there for purchasing cotton. We also have a ship's manifest of his travels to Havana, which we assume was to purchase sugar. As an ambitious, well-travelled businessman, Rudolph was well on his way in pursuing the American dream.

On June 15, 1835, Rudolph married Charlotte Elisabeth McCarthy Hossack. In the succeeding two years, Rudolph and Mary had two sons, Henri Monod (1836–1900) and Frederik August (1837–1851). Around this time, the family lived on Henry Street in Brooklyn Heights, a growing New York suburb

Brooklyn Heights, Where the Braëm Family Resided on Henry Street

where residents would commute to Manhattan or work in the Brooklyn Naval Yard.

In May 1838, Rudolph became a naturalized citizen of the United States. However, he passed away in October of that same year, leaving behind his widow and two young sons. We do not know the cause of his death and can only speculate that he succumbed to disease as there was a Cholera outbreak in NYC at the time. After his death, his widow, Charlotte, moved to Copenhagen with the two children and lived with Rudolph's brother, Captain Johan Braëm.

She later returned to New York with her sons and married another Dane, Edvard Bech (1812–1873) in 1846. Bech was a successful New York merchant who later founded the Tuckerman and Bech Iron Company and became

Charlotte Elizabeth McCarthy Braëm Beck
(1812 — 1900)

Danish Consul General in New York. He was also a partner in Cunard Steamship Company.

The family settled in Poughkeepsie where they raised the two boys with their four half-siblings. Bech died in 1873, leaving the family home, Rosenlund, to his widow. It was later sold to the Marist brothers and turned into Marist College. That same year, the eldest son, Henri Braëm, assumed his stepfather's role as Danish Consul General in New York.

Henri Braëm married Emily Maria Forbes in 1862 and had two daughters, Pauline (1871–1916) and Josephine (1874-1956). In 1875, Braëm built

Ethelwynde, a summer cottage in Lenox, Massachusetts where his family was celebrated in the New York society pages for their grand balls and other gala functions until 1898 when due to financial troubles he sold the house to the widow of Robert Winthrop.

Toward the end of the century, Henri moved to Vienna, Austria to live with his daughters who had married aristocratic Austrian army officers. At the age of 63, he died from pneumonia in Austria in 1900.

Rudolph Braëm's diary of his voyage to America has been shared within his brother Johan's family for generations. Johan's granddaughter Charlotte began translating the diary from Old Danish to modern Danish in the early 20th Century. In 2009, her great grandson, Donald Valade, had the diary translated by the Danish American Society in Iowa so it can be enjoyed by Braëm descendants in the United States as it teaches them about early 19th Century American history through the eyes of their ancestor.

"Since World War I, no one has heard of them, although my grandmother, Charlotte Vedel, corresponded with them until 1914. We have photographs of the two beautiful girls.

"In 2004, my cousin's son, David Valade, by searching the name Braëm over the internet, found and contacted Pauline's descendants in America. Rudolph's bloodline still exists, just as his memory does in our family."

Steen Vedel (Grandson of Charlotte Vede)
Excerpted from Steen's Original Prologue

1.

December 1829.

Rudolph Braëm's Diary

121

SLÆGTEN   BRAËM

www.ingramcontent.com/pod-product-compliance
Lightning Source LLC
Chambersburg PA
CBHW041957090426
42811CB00014B/1524